Renee F. Dawn 4

## ESSENTIAL ELEMENTS FOR CHOIR – BOOK TWO

# ESSENTIAL MUSICIANSHIP

## A COMPREHENSIVE CHORAL METHOD

### VOICE • THEORY • SIGHT-READING • PERFORMANCE

**BY**
**EMILY CROCKER**
**AND**
**JOHN LEAVITT**

*Essential Musicianship* Consultants and Authors of *Essential Repertoire*
Glenda Casey
Bobbie Douglass
Jan Juneau
Janice Killian
Michael O'Hern
Linda Rann
Brad White

### To the Student

Welcome to Essential Musicianship! We are pleased that you have chosen to participate in choral singing. With practice and dedication, you'll enjoy a lifetime of musical performance. Best wishes for your musical success!

ISBN 978-0-7935-4333-5

7777 W. BLUEMOUND RD. P.O. BOX 13819 MILWAUKEE, WI 53213

# CONTENTS

## TABLE OF CONTENTS AND OVERVIEW OF THE PROGRAM

ii

 **TABLE OF CONTENTS AND OVERVIEW OF THE PROGRAM**

## TABLE OF CONTENTS AND OVERVIEW OF THE PROGRAM

## TO THE TEACHER

This and the preceding Volume 1 and subsequent Volume 3 are designed to provide a basis for developing comprehensive musicianship within the choral rehearsal through a sequenced study of voice, music theory, and the practical application of both in music reading skills.

### Features of the Program

- The sequence is pedagogically sound and practical. The necessary elements for good choral singing are systematically presented.

- The terminology is accurate and literal.

- Vocal pedagogy and music theory are presented in a format that is ideal for introducing important musical concepts within the choral rehearsal.

- The method is designed to help students become independent thinkers and to constantly apply their learning to an ever-widening set of musical experiences.

- It provides a ready-made resource of choral concepts and repertoire presented in a practical sequence that is ideal for both beginning and experienced teachers.

- It is designed to be successful within a variety of choral organizations: treble, tenor bass, mixed.

- The concepts presented are structured to allow students to discover their individual potential. The material is score-oriented, i.e. the students are led to discover the meaning of music both through experiencing it and interpreting it through the medium of the printed page. This process of converting "symbol to sound" and "sound to symbol" is at the heart of becoming a musically literate individual.

### Combining ESSENTIAL MUSICIANSHIP with ESSENTIAL REPERTOIRE

This book may be presented in conjunction with any of the four levels of *ESSENTIAL REPERTOIRE*, twelve volumes of high quality, time-tested choral literature for mixed, treble, and tenor bass choirs.

For each choral selection in *ESSENTIAL REPERTOIRE*, the authors have provided complete lesson plans including:
- Objectives
- Historical/stylistic guidelines and cultural context
- Choral techniques (warm-ups, exercises, drills)
- Rehearsal and performance tips
- Assessment techniques and enrichment ideas

Together with *ESSENTIAL MUSICIANSHIP*, these books provide a complete curriculum for the choral experience.

## HOW TO USE THIS BOOK

Book 2 is organized into twenty segments (chapters), each including material for developing skills in voice, theory, sight-reading, and performance. If students have completed Book 1, Book 2 presents a review of concepts previously introduced, and extends the learning into additional new areas. Thus, if the students are older, or have some experience in choral singing, you may wish to begin with Book 2. (For example, if students have used Book 1 in Grades 7-8, use Book 2 in Grade 9.)

The material in each segment has been systematically developed to integrate all the skills of a choral musician. How long to remain within a single segment will depend on a variety of circumstances, including the age and experience level of the students and how often the group meets.

Allow approximately 15 minutes of a 1-hour rehearsal to be devoted to the "voice/theory/sight-reading" portions of this material. This need not be approached as a block section of the rehearsal, but can be integrated throughout the lesson in shorter sessions to heighten students' interest.

Each day's material should be balanced between review/practice and presenting new material. Before proceeding to the next chapter, evaluate the students' comprehension and mastery of the material.

### Voice
Each segment provides material to help a young singer learn and apply the techniques of good singing, and particularly emphasizes the importance of:
• Good posture
• Expanded rib cage breathing, breath support, learning to sustain a phrase
• Choral blend, vertical vowel formation, diphthongs, word stress
• Diction, articulation of consonants
• Registers, resonance

### Theory
Each segment presents music theory concepts in a clear and concise manner. Appropriate drill is included and "check your knowledge" questions are presented in each chapter for a quick evaluation of knowledge-based material. Specific concepts are highlighted at the top of each page and in the table of contents/sequence overview on p. ii.

### Sight-Reading
The sight-reading drills and exercises are designed to practice the concepts presented in the theory section of the chapter. Keep in mind that as the students practice particular drills they are internalizing that aural skill and synthesizing it with other musical concepts they have experienced.

## HOW TO USE THIS BOOK

(continued)

The sight-reading drills include:
- Basic familiarity with musical terms and symbols
- Note identification
- Drills for echo-singing and group practice
- Combinable exercises that provide practice in unison sight-reading and part-singing

When working on the sight-reading material, always be musical when demonstrating and performing a particular phrase or pattern. Apply sight-reading skills in every area of music-making.

### Performance

Each chapter includes repertoire that applies and reinforces the concepts presented in each chapter. These songs, written for treble, tenor bass, and mixed ensembles provide:
- Resources for developing reading skills, and the application of musical concepts.
- Resources for developing musicianship and expressive singing.
- Concert level repertoire that includes quality texts, a balance of styles, harmonic, melodic and rhythmic aspects of music-making (canons, counterpoint, expressive and satisfying melodies, speech choruses), and interesting musical forms.
- A balance of repetition/patterning and experience with more challenging material.

### Music History

Throughout the text, short informational sections are included to help put the material presented into a historical context. This supplementary material helps students to see their own role as choral musicians now and as a part of a rich and rewarding tradition.

### Methods of Sight-Reading

There are many good methods to use in developing sight-reading skills. They all have advantages and drawbacks. In selecting a method to follow, consider the following:
- Age and experience of the singers
- Methods used by other musical organizations in your school or district
- Methods familiar to your students
- Your own background and training

Remember, it is not which method you choose, but rather that it is employed consistently and daily.

An overview of several common sight-reading methods for both pitch and rhythm are described in the appendix, beginning on page 213.

A teacher's edition is available for each of the three volumes of *ESSENTIAL MUSICIANSHIP*. It includes a more complete overview of the course, and detailed lesson plans for presenting the material. See page 228 for a full series listing.

## POSTURE/BREATH

**Posture:** A good singing posture helps produce good breathing for singing. An effective singing posture includes the following:
- Stand with feet apart
- Knees unlocked
- Back straight
- Head erect
- Rib cage lifted
- Shoulders relaxed
- Hands at your side

Standing posture          Raising the rib cage

1. To help develop good posture for singing, practice this exercise: Place your fingertips on the crown of your head (elbows out). Notice how your rib cage is raised. Slowly open your arms and continue in a downward arc until they rest at your sides. Try to maintain the raised rib cage as you lower your arms.

**Breath:** An expanded rib cage increases breath capacity and provides the basis for a free, relaxed and pleasing vocal tone. The following exercise will help you expand the rib cage and take a full breath for singing.

2. Raise your arms overhead slowly while inhaling, then exhale your air on a "ss" while slowly lowering your arms to their original position. Try to maintain the raised rib cage while lowering your arms.

3. Repeat #2, but this time exhale on 4 short "ss" sounds followed by a longer "ss."

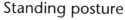

ss  ss  ss  ss  ss_____(repeat once or twice in one breath)

4. Imagine there is a milkshake as large as the room. Hold your arms out from your body like you were holding the giant milkshake and "drink" the air through a giant straw. Exhale.

## TONE

**Tone:** While you use your voice everyday for communication, singing requires a different way of producing a sound. A *"yawn-sigh"* is a very useful exercise that helps prepare the voice to produce a full relaxed, free, and pleasing tone.

5. Yawn-sigh-yawn, then starting on a high pitch, produce a relaxed, descending vocal sigh on an "ah" vowel, somewhat like a siren.

**Vowels:**

Vowels are the basis for a good choral tone, so make sure that you sing all your vowels with a *relaxed jaw*, a *vertical mouth shape*, and *space inside your mouth*. This helps each singer to produce a full and free vocal tone quality that blends well with other voices to create a pleasing choral sound.

The *five basic vowel*s include:

| ee | eh | ah | oh | oo |

Notice that each is produced with a relaxed and vertical dropped jaw. Practice the following exercises based on the 5 basic vowels.

⑥ yah yah yah yah yah yah yah

⑦ mee ___ meh ___ mah ___ moh ___ moo

 **RHYTHM**

*Rhythm* is the organization of sound length (duration).

*Beat* is a steadily recurring pulse.

For practice, keep a steady beat as a group. Clap, tap, or chant with a clock or metronome.

**Note values**
Three common note values are the *quarter* note, the *half* note, and the *whole* note.

Quarter note      Half note      Whole note

In most of the music that we'll begin with, the quarter note will be assigned the beat.

You'll notice from the chart that *two quarter notes* have the same duration as *one half note*, and that *two half notes (or four quarter notes)* have the same duration as *one whole note*.

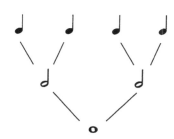

**Check your knowledge!**
1. What is *rhythm*?

2. What is *beat*?

3. Identify the following notes:

4. How many quarter notes equal the same duration as a half note?

5. How many half notes equal the same duration as a whole note?

6. How many quarter notes equal the same duration as a whole note?

**RHYTHM PRACTICE**

Read each line (clap, tap, or chant). Concentrate on keeping a steady beat. Repeat as necessary until you've mastered the exercise.

① ♩ ♩ ♩ ♩ | ♩ ♩ ♩ ♩ | ♩ ♩ ♩ ♩ | ♩ ♩ ♩ ♩
    1  2  3  4   1  2  3  4   1  2  3  4   1  2  3  4

② ♩    ♩ | ♩    ♩ | ♩    ♩ | ♩    ♩
    1     3   1     3   1     3   1     3

③ 𝅝 | 𝅝 | 𝅝 | 𝅝
   1      1      1      1

④ ♩ ♩ ♩ ♩ | ♩    ♩ | ♩ ♩ ♩ ♩ | ♩    ♩
    1  2  3  4   1     3   1  2  3  4   1     3

⑤ ♩ ♩ ♩ | ♩ ♩ ♩ | ♩    ♩ | 𝅝
    1  2  3   1  2  3   1     3   1

⑥ ♩  ♩ ♩ | ♩  ♩ ♩ | ♩ ♩ ♩ ♩ | 𝅝
    1    3  4   1    3  4   1  2  3  4   1

⑦ 𝅝 | ♩ ♩ ♩ ♩ | 𝅝 | ♩ ♩ ♩ ♩
   1      1  2  3  4   1         1  2  3  4

⑧ ♩    ♩ | 𝅝 | ♩    ♩ | 𝅝
    1     3   1      1     3   1

### BASIC NOTATION

A *staff* is a graph of 5 lines and 4 spaces on which music is written. The staff shown below is a *grand staff*. A grand staff is a grouping of two staves.

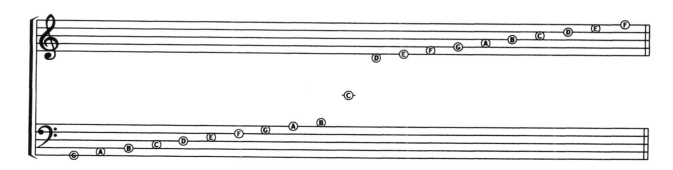

**Notes on the Keyboard**

lower ⟵ Middle C ⟶ higher

Notice the two symbols at the beginning of the staves on the left hand side. These are called clefs. A *clef* is a symbol that identifies a set of pitches. The *Treble Clef* generally refers to pitches higher than middle C. The *Bass Clef* generally refers to pitches lower than middle C. Notice that middle C has its own little line and may be written in either clef at the bottom of the treble or the top of the bass clef.

- Treble Clef (G clef)
- Second line is G
  (The curve of the clef
  loops around the G line)

- Bass Clef (F clef)
- Fourth line is F
  (The dots of the clef surround
  the F line.)

An easy way to learn the notes on the treble clef staff is to remember that the spaces spell the word *FACE* from the bottom up. An easy way to learn the notes on the bass clef staff is to remember that the spaces spell *ACEG* or *All Cows Eat Grass*. Make up your own phrase for the acronym *GBDFA* (for the bass clef lines) and *EGBDF* (for the treble clef lines).

## NOTE IDENTIFICATION PRACTICE

### Check your knowledge!

1.  What is the name of the graph of lines and spaces on which music is written?

2.  How many lines and spaces does this graph have?

3.  What is the name of the symbol used to describe a set of pitches?

4.  Name two types of these symbols.

5.  Name the pitch which may be written on its own little line in either clef.

### Practice

Name the notes in the following examples.

### PRACTICE-NOTE IDENTIFICATION

Practice echo-singing these notes by letter name.

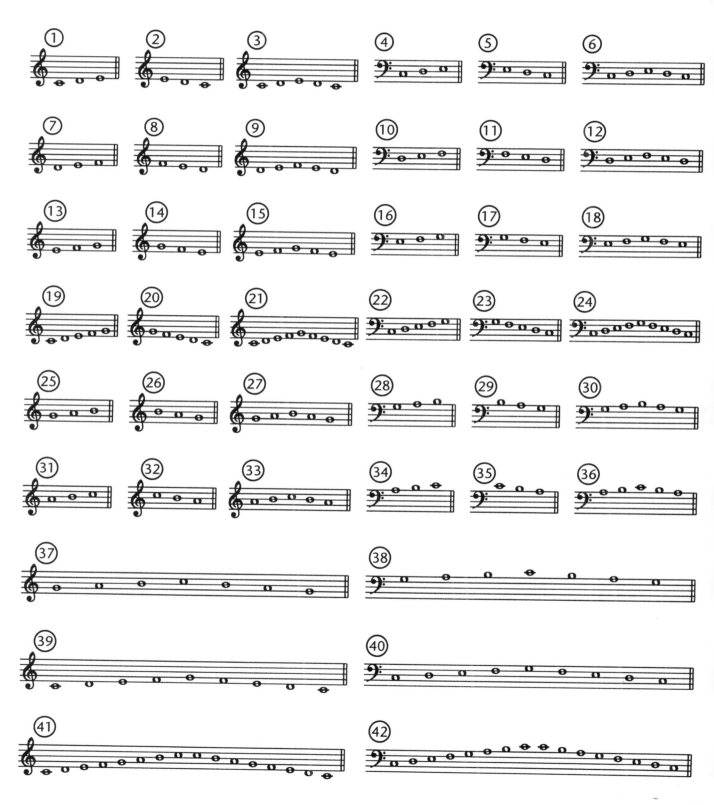

## POSTURE/BREATH

**Posture:** Review the steps to a good singing posture:
- Stand with feet apart
- Knees unlocked
- Back straight
- Head erect
- Rib cage lifted
- Shoulders relaxed
- Hands at your side

**Breath:** Remember that a lifted and expanded rib cage helps to develop expanded breath capacity. When you sing a musical phrase supported by a good singing breath, you are demonstrating good breath support.

1. Bend at the waist and pick an imaginary flower. Inhale the "fragrance" while slowly standing up. Exhale on a yawn-sigh.

2. Put your hands on the sides of your rib cage and inhale. Notice the movement of the rib cage. Breathe out on a whispered "ah."

**Diaphragmatic Breathing:** One aspect of breath support is the lifted and expanded rib cage. Another aspect of breath support is the process of activating the *diaphragm*. The diaphragm is a muscle just below the lungs that moves downward during inhalation as the rib cage expands and air fills the lungs. Exercises which help you become aware of this action of the diaphragm can help you learn to energize and enrich the vocal sound you are producing.

3. When people are surprised or frightened, they usually take in a rapid breath with a noticeable movement of the diaphragm. Place your hand just below your rib cage and above your waist and then take a "surprised breath."
   - Do you feel the movement?
   - Did your hand move as a result of the surprised breath?

4. See if you can produce the same movement of the diaphragm as in #3 in the following exercise. Use short *whispered* sounds, no voice.

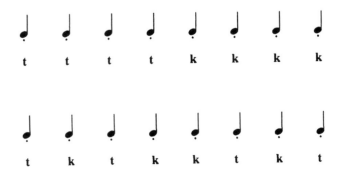

 **BREATH/TONE**

5. Practice the following exercise keeping the sounds short and detached. Use the diaphragm as in #4 to support and energize the tone. Remember to produce the vowel sounds with a relaxed jaw, vertical mouth position, and space inside the mouth. Repeat at different pitch levels, both higher and lower.

6. In the following exercise, sing the musical pitches so they are smooth and connected.

Take a full expanded rib cage breath supported by the action of the diaphragm (even though in this exercise the notes are connected and not short). Produce the vowels with a relaxed jaw, vertical mouth shape and space inside the mouth.

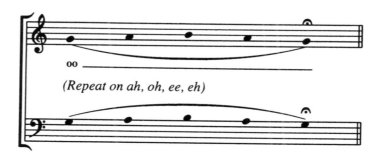

7. In the following exercise connect two notes together on the syllable "moh." Be sure that your vowel does not change as you prepare to sing the next "m."

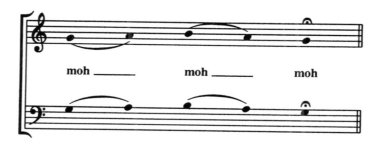

## MEASURES • METERS • BARLINES

*Barlines* are vertical lines that divide the staff into smaller sections called *measures*. A *double barline* indicates the end of a section or piece of music.

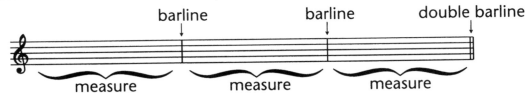

*Meter* is a form of rhythmic organization. For example:

4 = Four beats per measure ( ♩ ♩ ♩ ♩ )
4 = The quarter note ( ♩ ) receives the beat.

3 = Three beats per measure ( ♩ ♩ ♩ )
4 = The quarter note ( ♩ ) receives the beat.

2 = Two beats per measure ( ♩ ♩ )
4 = The quarter note ( ♩ ) receives the beat.

The numbers that identify the meter are called the *time signature*. The time signature is placed after the clef at the beginning of a song or section of a song.

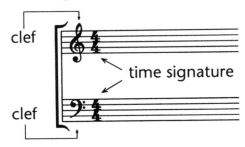

### Check your knowledge!

1. What are the vertical lines that divide a staff into smaller sections called?

2. Name the smaller divided sections of a staff.

3. What is a *double barline*?

4. Describe *meter*.

5. What are the numbers that identify the meter called?

6. Describe the following meters:  4/4   3/4   2/4

**RHYTHM PRACTICE**

Clap, tap or chant.

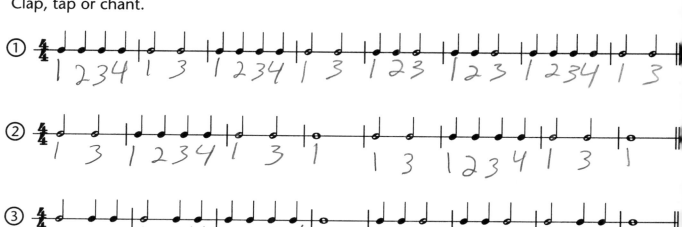

## PITCH • SCALE • KEY OF C

*Pitch* is the highness or lowness of musical sound. It is another name for the musical notes that we write on a staff.

A *scale* is an inventory or collection of pitches. The word *scale* comes from the Italian *scala* meaning "ladder." Thus, many musical scales are a succession of pitches higher and/or lower.

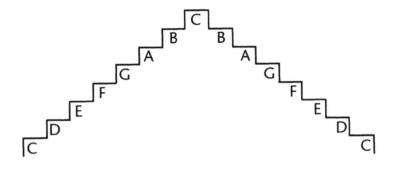

*Key* is the importance of one pitch over the others in a scale. The key note or tone might be described as the home tone. In the Key of C, C is the home tone or keynote.

Key of C Scale

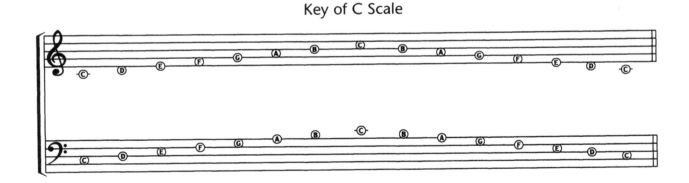

**Practice:** After listening to your teacher sing (or play) the C scale, try singing the C scale.

### Check your knowledge!
1. What is another name for musical notes?

2. Define *scale*. Define *scala*.

3. Describe *key*. Describe *keynote*.

## KEY OF C PRACTICE

Identify the following pitches in the key of C. Echo-sing these drills, or sing as a group.

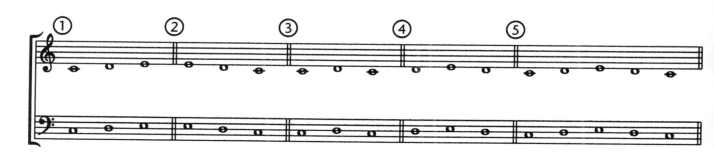

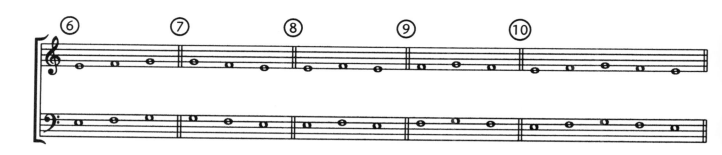

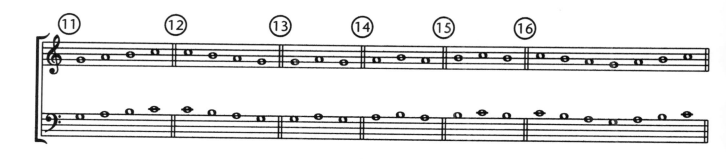

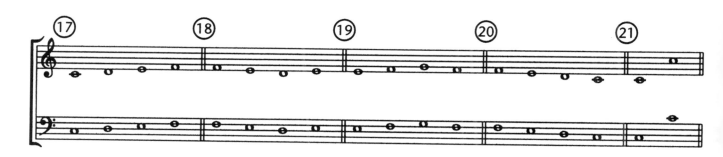

## RHYTHM AND PITCH PRACTICE

The following exercises combine rhythm and pitch.  Read the rhythm first, then add the pitch.
Repeat as needed for accuracy.

① Do re me fa Sol Fa me Re Do  DO Re me Re Do

② DO  Do Re me Fa Sol  Sol Fa  me Fa me

③ Do  Do Re me Fa Sol  Sol Fa me  me Re Do

④ Do  Do DO  Do Re Do  Do Re me Fa Sol Sol

⑤ La te Do Re me Re Do te  La  La Sol  La Sol me

⑥ La  La te Do Re  me  me Re

⑦

⑧

### UNISON VOICES

For extra challenge, here is a short song with piano accompaniment.
- The piece begins with two measures of piano accompaniment.
- In this piece, the vocal lines are indicated by arrows: →
- Sight-read the rhythm, then add the pitch. Repeat as needed.
- Add the printed text, then add the piano accompaniment. The voices enter on a C independent of the piano. Practice until you can enter on the keynote.
- This piece uses slurs, i.e. in measure 4, notice the curved line connecting two notes of different pitch. A slur means to sing the notes smoothly on the same word or syllable.
- Take full, expanded rib cage breaths and sing vertical vowels.

# Sweet Music In The Night
For Unison voices and Piano

Words and Music by
EMILY CROCKER

## POSTURE/BREATH/TONE

**Posture:** Check your posture and ask yourself these questions.
- Stand with feet apart (Is your weight balanced?)
- Knees unlocked (Can you bend them easily?)
- Back straight (Are you standing erect comfortably and not stiff?)
- Head erect (Is your chin level, and not too far up or down?)
- Rib cage lifted (Is your chest high and able to expand?)
- Shoulders relaxed (Are they comfortably down, not too far forward or back?)
- Hands at your side (Are they relaxed and free of tension?)

Just like athletes, singers need to prepare themselves for the physical process of singing. Performance, whether on the playing field or in a concert, will suffer if the body is not sufficiently prepared or involved.

Practice good posture, good breathing, and good vocal habits every day in rehearsal, and these good habits will be there to help you succeed in performance.

1. Lift the left shoulder high and then let it fall. Repeat with the right shoulder and then both shoulders. Drop the head gently to the chest, and then let it roll to the right and then the left. Stretch overhead, then fall forward like a rag doll and gradually stand up to a good singing posture.

**Breath:** Practice breathing exercises every day. Apply this practice to all your music making, sight-reading music, rehearsing music, performing music.

2. When people are suddenly startled, they usually take a deep natural breath very quickly. Take a "surprised" breath. Notice the action of the *diaphragm.*

3. Imagine that there is an elevator platform at the bottom of your lungs. Drop the platform toward the floor as you inhale. Inhale 4 counts, exhale 4 counts. Repeat with 5, then 6 counts.

**Tone:** Review the 5 basic vowels used in choral singing: ee, eh, ah, oh, oo. Most other vowel sounds are modifications or blends of these five sounds.

ee      eh      ah      oh      oo

## TONE

4. Practice the following exercise and notice the difference between the vowels. With all the vowels remember to keep a relaxed jaw and vertical space inside the mouth.

Especially on the "ee" and "eh" vowels, it is important to keep the corners of the mouth from spreading outward. If you sing the "ee" and "eh" vowels with a horizontal rather than a vertical mouth shape, they may sound flat and disrupt the tone quality you are trying to achieve.
* For the "ee" vowel, keep the corners of your mouth tucked in.
* For the "eh" vowel, the mouth is opened slightly more than the "ee."
* For both, use space inside the mouth.
* Repeat the exercise at different pitch levels, both higher and lower.

5. Practice the following descending scale.
* Take an expanded rib cage breath and try to sing the entire pattern on one breath.
* Keep a relaxed jaw and vertical space inside your mouth. Keep the corners of your mouth from spreading outward.
* Change smoothly from one vowel to the next. Blend your voice with those around you.
* Repeat at different pitch levels, both higher and lower.

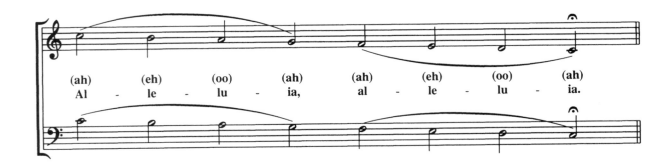

## REVIEW

### Check your knowledge!

1. What is the name of the graph of lines and spaces upon which music is written?

2. How many lines and spaces does this graph have?

3. What is *musical pitch*?

4. What is the name of the symbol used to describe a set of pitches? Name two types of these symbols.

5. Give another name for G clef. Give another name for F clef. Describe both clefs.

6. Name the pitch which may be written on its own little line in either clef.

7. What is *rhythm*?

8. What is a steady recurring pulse called?

9. Identify the following notes: ♩  ♩  𝅝

10. How many quarter notes equal a whole note? How many half notes equal a whole note?

11. Define *barline* and *measure*.

12. What symbol is used to signal the end of a piece of music?

13. Name a form of rhythmic organization.

14. What is a time signature? Name and describe three time signatures.

15. Describe *key*. Describe *keynote*.

16. What is a *scale*? What does the Italian word *scala* mean?

### WHOLE STEPS · HALF STEPS

Remember that *key* is the importance of one pitch over the others in a scale. The keynote is described as the home tone. So far, we've learned the *key of C*, which if played on the piano would begin on C and progress stepwise using only the white keys of the piano.

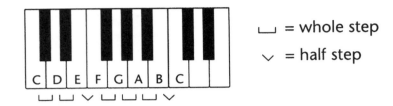

⌐⌐ = whole step

∨ = half step

These steps on the piano for the key of C are an arrangement of *whole steps* and *half steps*.

A *half step* is the smallest distance (or *interval*) between two notes on a keyboard.

A *whole step* is the combination of two half steps side by side.

A *major scale* is a specific arrangement of whole steps and half steps in the following order:

C Major Scale

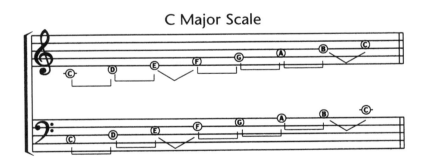

### Check your knowledge!

1. What is a *half step*? What is a *whole step*?

2. What is a *major scale*?

3. What is the order of whole/half steps in a major scale?

**WHOLE/HALF STEP PRACTICE**

## SINGING IN PARTS

**History:** Human voices are generally divided into four basic ranges:
soprano - the highest treble voice, usually written in treble clef
alto - a treble voice that is lower than the soprano, usually written in treble clef
tenor - a male voice written in bass clef or treble clef
bass - a male voice written in bass clef that is lower than a tenor voice

The following exercises combine pitch and rhythm. Read each line separately, repeating as needed for accuracy. When you've mastered all the lines, you may sing them in any combination. Each line sung by itself produces *melody* (a succession of musical tones). When two or more melodies are combined, the result is *harmony* (musical tones sounded simultaneously).

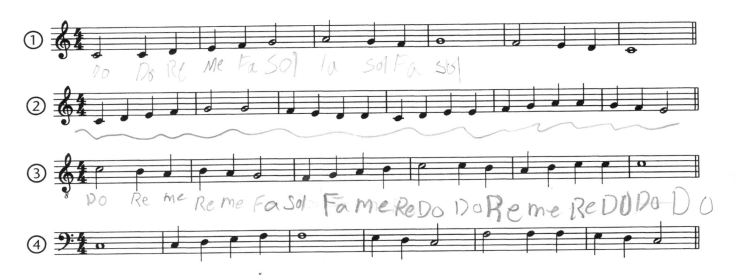

In the music below, lines #1 through #3 which you have just sung, are combined. Notice how the parts are bracketed together.

## PITCH PRACTICE

Remember that middle C can be written on its own short line in either clef. Other pitches may be written that way also. These short lines are called *ledger lines*. Ledger lines may be used to represent notes either above or below the staff. In the following graphic, notes connected by arrows are the same pitch.

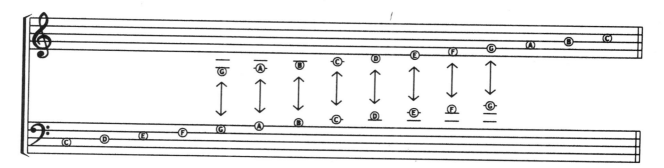

Practice the following patterns. Echo-sing or sing as a group.

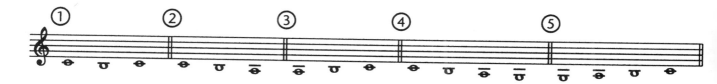

### MORE PITCH PRACTICE

In the music below, 2 or more lines are bracketed together. Sing the exercises separately and together as they are bracketed.

 **TREBLE • TENOR BASS • MIXED**

Remember the four basic ranges of the human voice: soprano, alto, tenor, bass.

Note: When the tenor part is written in treble clef, there is sometimes a small "8" attached to the clef sign. This means that the notes are to be sung 1 octave (8 notes) lower. Even when the "8" is missing from the clef sign, tenors sing an octave lower. For example:

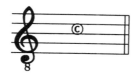 sounds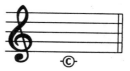

The three choral pieces on pages 26-29 were written for three different types of choral *ensembles*. An *ensemble* is a French term, and refers to a group of musicians performing together.
• Treble Chorus (soprano and alto)
• Tenor Bass Chorus (tenor and bass)
• Mixed Chorus (soprano, alto, tenor, bass)

**Musical terms:** *Dynamics* refers to the degree of loudness or softness in performing music. In the 18th century a new instrument was developed in Italy called the *pianoforte*, an Italian term meaning "soft-loud." It was called this because unlike an earlier instrument called the *harpsichord*, the loudness of the piano's sound could be varied by the touch of the fingers. Later the name of the instrument was shortened to *piano*. Now, dynamics still usually are written with their Italian names or as abbreviations:

*p* - *piano*; soft

*mp* - *mezzo-piano*; medium soft

*mf* - *mezzo-forte*; medium loud

*f* - *forte*; loud

As you prepare to perform the following songs:
• Identify the vocal lines.
• Read the rhythm, then add the pitch.
• Add the text and repeat as necessary to become accurate.
• Take full expanded rib cage breaths and sing with vertical vowels.

**TREBLE CHORUS**

# Indian Summer

For SA or SSA a cappella

Text by
JOHN GREENLEAF WHITTIER

Music by
EMILY CROCKER

## TENOR BASS CHORUS

The text of this song is one of hundreds dealing with love and love's misfortune. In this particular text, the song tells of all the terrible things that will happen if the singer does not remain true to the one he loves.

# Love's Lament
### For TB or TTB a cappella

**Text:**
**Traditional Folksong**

**Music by**
**EMILY CROCKER**

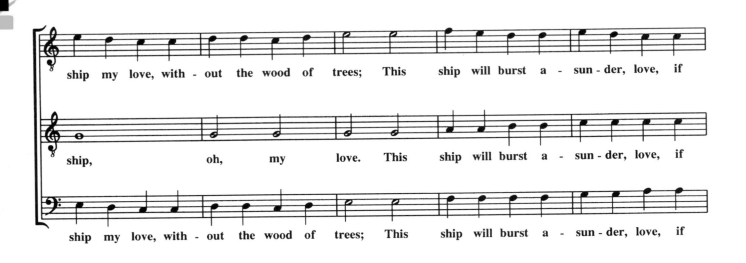

ship my love, with - out the wood of trees; This ship will burst a - sun - der, love, if

ship, oh, my love. This ship will burst a - sun - der, love, if

ship my love, with - out the wood of trees; This ship will burst a - sun - der, love, if

I prove false to you. If I prove false to you, the rocks will

I prove false to you. If I prove false to you, the rocks will melt and

I prove false to you, to you. If I prove false to you, the rocks will

run, The fire will freeze through out, my love, the rag - ing sea will burn.

Opt. div.

run, The fire will freeze through out, my love, the rag - ing sea __ will burn.

melt and run, The fire will freeze through out, my love, the rag - ing sea __ will burn.

## MIXED CHORUS

The Greek words *Kyrie eleison, Christe eleison* became common in the Latin mass dating from about the 9th century. After about 1600, composers became interested in the musical form inherent in the mass setting, and the great masses of Bach, Haydn, and others are often performed as concert works in secular contexts. Pronunciation: KEE-ree-eh eh-LEH-ee-sohn

# Kyrie Eleison
For SATB a cappella

Music by
JOHN LEAVITT

## POSTURE/BREATH

1. Stretch overhead, side to side, up and down, then shake to relax any tight muscles.

2. Raise your arms overhead, stretching the fingers out in all directions. Bring the arms back to the side, relaxed and free of tension.

3. Exhale all your air. Wait for a moment until your body lets you know it needs air. Allow the air to flow in without effort. Repeat.

4. Imagine you have a milkshake as large as the room. Hold your arms in front of you around this giant "milkshake" and drink in the air through a giant "straw."

5. Place your fingertips just below your rib cage and take a "surprised" breath. Notice the movement of the diaphragm.

6. Inhale while raising your arms overhead (notice the expanded rib cage). Exhale on a hiss in this pattern, while slowly lowering your arms:

    ss  ss  ss  ss  ss_____(repeat 1 or 2 times on each breath)

### Articulation

We have concentrated on vowel sounds so far (ee, eh, ah, oh, oo). Singing text requires *articulation* to produce the consonants. The *articulators* that we use in vocal music are the teeth, the lips, and the tongue.

7. For practice, repeat this short phrase quickly and precisely, concentrating on clean and clear articulation:

*The lips, the teeth, the tip of the tongue...the lips, the teeth, the tip of the tongue...etc.*

Now sing the above phrase on a unison pitch. Produce good articulation without distorting the vertical vowel sound of each word.

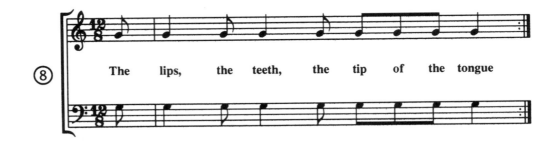

**TONE**

As you practice the following exercises, remember
- Keep a relaxed jaw and vertical space inside the mouth.
- Don't let the corners of the mouth spread outward.
- Listen, tune and blend your voice with other voices around you.
- Take a full, expanded rib cage breath before each repetition.
- A fermata ( 𝄐 ) means to hold that pitch longer than its normal duration, until your director signals you to release.
- In #10 and #11, clearly articulate the underlined consonants.
- Repeat at different pitch levels, both higher and lower.

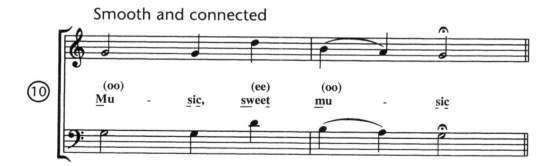

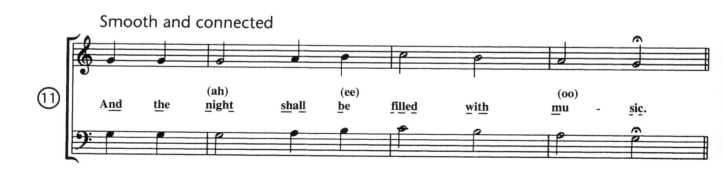

### SHARPS & FLATS • REVIEW OF C MAJOR

You'll recall the order of whole/half steps for the C major scale:

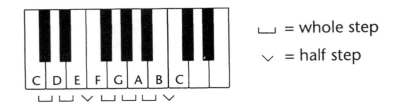

    ⊔ = whole step

    ∨ = half step

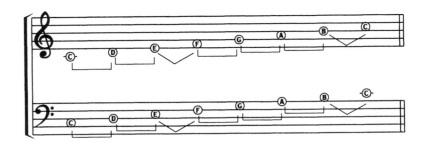

Music may be written with any note being the keynote. Because the order of whole/half steps must always be followed regardless of the keynote, the need arises for *sharps* ( ♯ ) and *flats* ( ♭ ).

A *sharp* [music] raises the pitch one half step. This note F♯ (F sharp) would be written with the sharp sign to the left of the notehead.

A *flat* [music] lowers the pitch one half step. This note B♭ (B flat) would be written with the flat sign to the left of the notehead.

### Practice:
Name the following pitches:

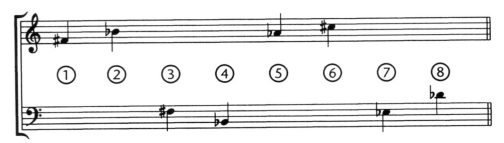

## SHARPS & FLATS • KEY OF G MAJOR

To build a major scale starting on G, using the same arrangement of whole steps and half steps as in the Key of C, you'll notice the need for an F♯.

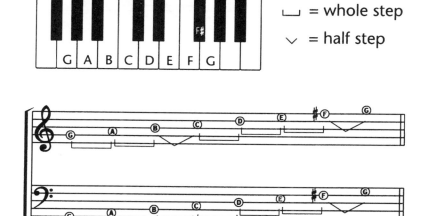

⊔ = whole step

⌄ = half step

If we had written F - G, the *interval* (distance) between these two pitches would have been a whole step rather than the required half step.

### Check your knowledge!
1. What is the order of whole/half steps for any major scale?

2. Does a *sharp* raise or lower a pitch? By how much?

3. Does a *flat* raise or lower a pitch? By how much?

### Key of G Practice
Practice singing the key of G scale. Three octaves of the G scale are written below. Because of the wider range, you'll only be able to sing a portion of the three *octaves*, but take note of your own vocal range. What is your lowest note? Your highest note?

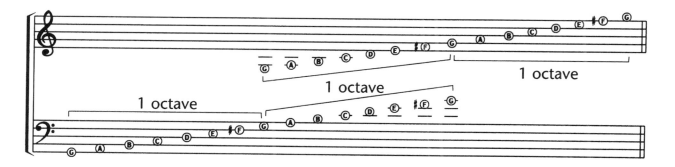

## KEY OF G PRACTICE

Identify the following pitches in the key of G. Echo-sing or sing as a group.

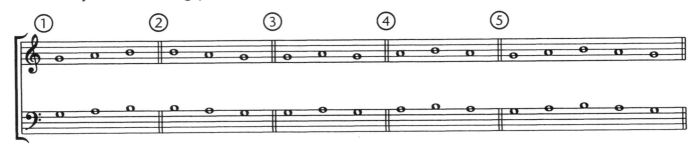

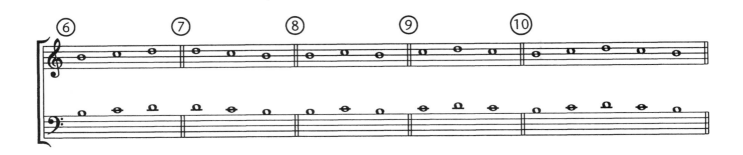

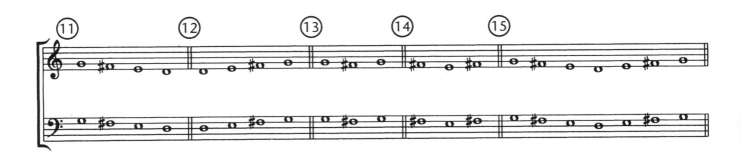

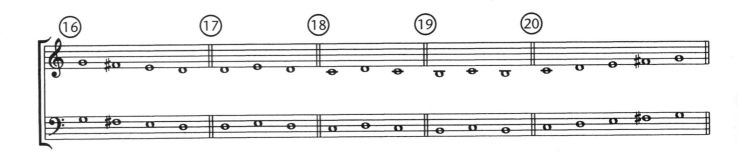

## ACCIDENTALS · KEY SIGNATURE

Let's review sharps and flats.

A *sharp* 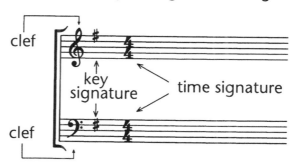 raises the pitch one half step. This note, F♯ (F sharp), would be written with the sharp sign to the left of the notehead.

A *flat* lowers the pitch one half step. This note, B♭ (B flat), would be written with the flat sign to the left of the notehead.

There are two ways to write sharps and flats in music. One way is to write the sharp or flat to the left of the notehead as shown above. These are called *accidentals* because they are not normally found in the key in which you are performing.

The other way is to write a *key signature*. Since we know that the key of G will always use an F♯, rather than write the sharp sign on every F in the song, we simply write a sharp on F's line at the beginning of the song right after the clef sign(s) and before the time signature. (Note: The key signature is used with every clef sign in the song as a reminder.)

clef

key signature          time signature

clef

Placing an F♯ in the key signature indicates that the music is in the key of *G major* which always uses an F♯. Remember that the key of *C major* has no sharps or flats. Thus, the absence of sharps or flats in the key signature indicates that the music is in the key of C major.

## Check your knowledge!
1. What is an *accidental*?

2. Where is a *sharp* or *flat* sign placed for a single note?

3. Where is a *key signature* placed?

4. What is the key signature for C major? For G major?

## KEY OF G PRACTICE

Sing each line separately and in any combination. Notice that not every melody starts on the keynote G. Identify the starting pitch of each melody and sing up or down the scale to locate the starting pitch.

**TREBLE • TENOR BASS • MIXED**

**Music History**

A *canon* is a musical form in which a melody in one part is followed a short time later by other parts performing the same melody. Sometimes the difference in time is as short as 1 beat. Other times it may be several measures. Canons are sometimes called *rounds*, and you may know several already: "Row, Row Your Boat," "Are You Sleeping," etc.

Canons are interesting musical forms because the *melody*, entering at staggered intervals, produces *harmony* when several voices are combined. This combination of voices in music is sometimes called *texture*. The earliest known canon dates to the 13th century and is called *Sumer is icumen in* ("Summer is a-coming in").

"Sun Is High" is a canon. As you learn this canon, follow this procedure:
*   Chant the rhythm of the unison melody, then add pitch. Repeat as needed to become secure. Add the text.
*   Combine the four parts as a canon.
*   Sing musically with rhythmic precision and good tone quality.

# Sun Is High

For 4-Part Canon a cappella

Text by
LOWELL MASON (1850)

Music by
JOHN LEAVITT

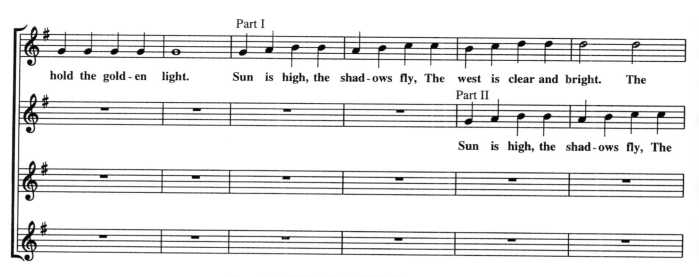

## POSTURE/BREATH

1. Lift the left shoulder high and then let it fall.  Repeat with the right shoulder and then both shoulders. Drop the head gently to the chest and then let it roll to the right and then the left.  Stretch overhead, fall forward like a rag doll and then gradually stand up to a good singing posture.

2. Imagine a balloon is attached to the top of your head.  Allow it to lift your head until it is in alignment with your spine and your rib cage is lifted.

3. Sniff in air 2 times quickly, then puff out 2 times quickly.
   Sniff 3, puff 3
   Sniff 4, puff 4
   Sniff 4, puff 2
   Sniff 2, puff 4

Notice how the air in your lungs feels buoyant.  Try to maintain this buoyant feeling of breath support as you sing the following vocalises.

**Tone/Articulation:** In each of the following exercises remember to:

* Maintain a good singing posture.
* Take a full expanded rib cage breath before each repetition.
* Activate the *articulators* (lips, teeth, tongue).
* Produce good tone by concentrating on vowel formation and vertical space inside the mouth.
* Repeat at different pitch levels, both higher and lower.

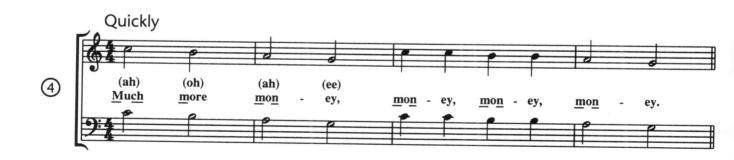

This exercise concentrates on "tip-of-the-tongue" consonants.  Sing it quickly, lightly, and without a lot of jaw movement.

In the following exercise the "st" sounds of "first" and "star" should merge together to maintain a smooth legato phrase.

Never prolong the "s" into a hiss.  Move quickly on to the next vowel or consonant.

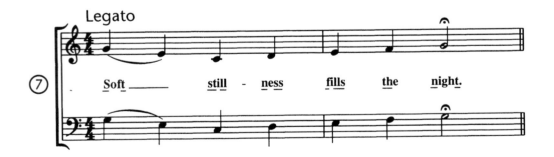

### MELODIC INTERVALS

An *interval* is the measurement of distance between two pitches. When intervals are played in succession, they are called *melodic intervals*. Following are examples of intervals of 2nds, 3rds, 4ths, and 5ths.

Read the pitches, echo sing, or sing each example as a group:

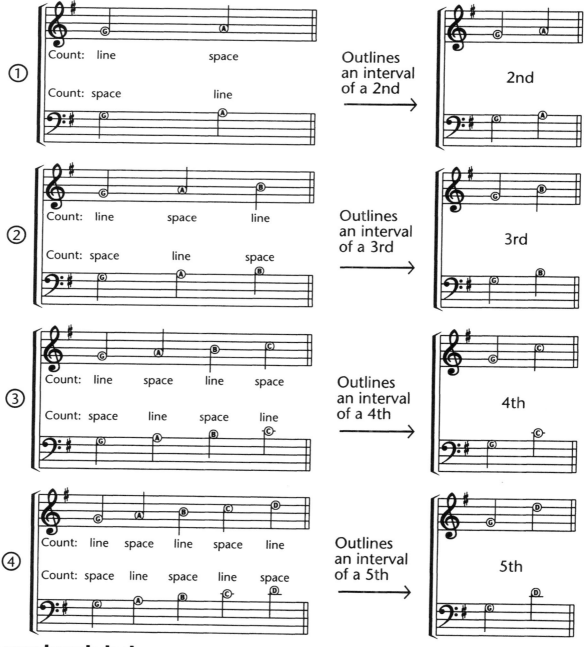

**Check your knowledge!**

1. What is an *interval*?

2. What are intervals played in succession called?

## MELODIC INTERVAL PRACTICE

Identify the following intervals.

Sing the following interval drills.

**KEY OF G INTERVAL PRACTICE**

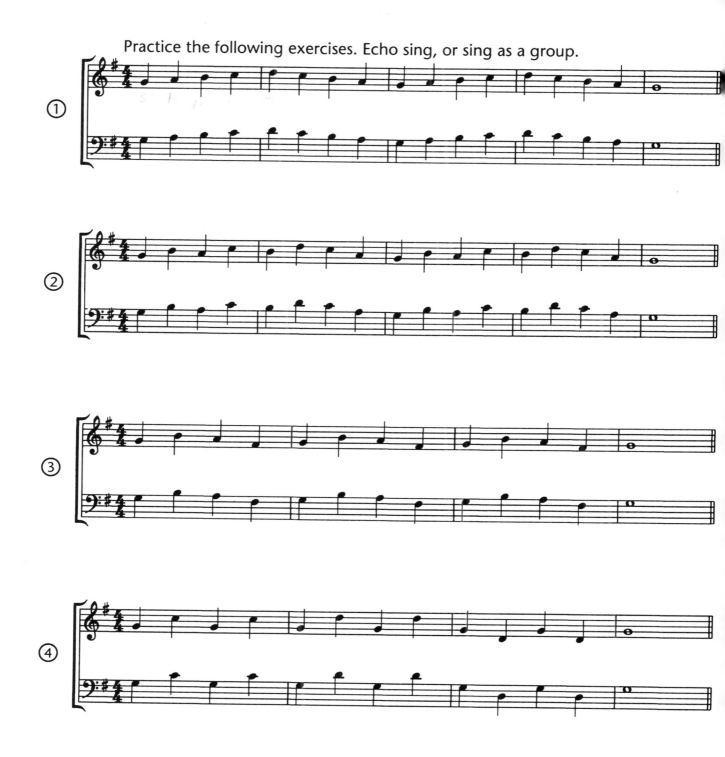

## HARMONIC INTERVALS

Earlier in this chapter, we learned that an *interval* is the measurement between two pitches. When intervals are played in succession, they are called *melodic intervals*.

When intervals are played simultaneously, they are called *harmonic* intervals. Here are some examples of harmonic intervals.

*Harmonic intervals* are the building blocks of harmony. Two or more harmonic intervals combined form a *chord*. Thus, a *chord* is the combination of 3 or more tones sounded simultaneously. Here are some examples of chords:

### Check your knowledge!
1. What are intervals played simultaneously called?

2. What are intervals played in succession called?

3. What is a *chord*?

## PRACTICE WITH INTERVALS

Practice the following exercises. Notice the harmonic intervals that result when one group sustains a pitch while the other group moves to a higher or lower pitch. Listen carefully for balance, tuning, and blend.

Notice the fermatas!

Practice the following exercises in 3 parts. Notice the chord that results as one group sustains a pitch while 2 other groups move higher and lower.

**MELODY AND HARMONY**

## TREBLE • TENOR BASS • MIXED

### Musical Terms

\> accent; emphasis on one note (or chord) over others around it. When singing a note that is accented, you can emphasize the note by singing it louder or by stressing the beginning consonant or vowel that starts the word. You can also use the diaphragm to create a breath accent.

*tempo* - speed of the beat.

*accel.* - *accelerando*; Italian term meaning to become faster; a gradual increase in tempo.

*al fine* - Italian terms meaning "to the end." Thus, *accel. al fine* means "gradually faster to the end."

# The Spider And The Fly

For SA, TB or SATB and Piano

Traditional text, adapted

Music by
EMILY CROCKER

47

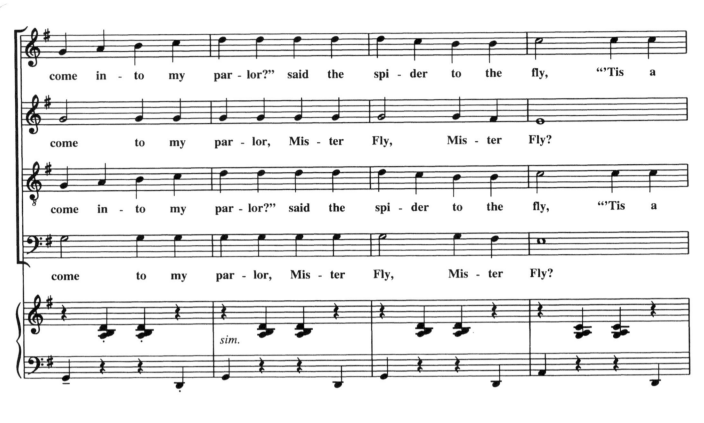

come in-to my par-lor?" said the spi-der to the fly, "'Tis a

come to my par-lor, Mis-ter Fly, Mis-ter Fly?

come in-to my par-lor?" said the spi-der to the fly, "'Tis a

come to my par-lor, Mis-ter Fly, Mis-ter Fly?

*sim.*

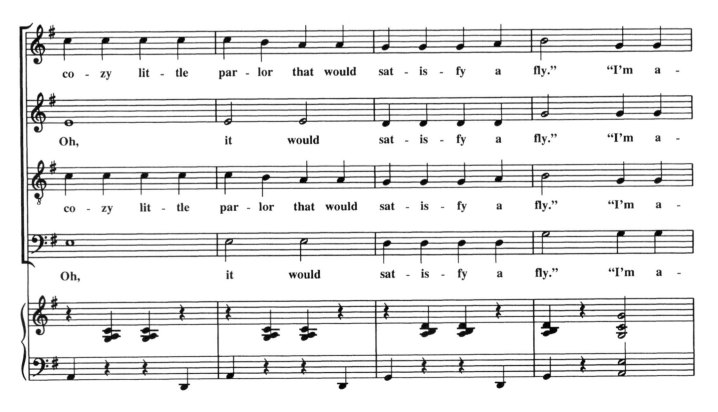

co - zy lit - tle par - lor that would sat - is - fy a fly." "I'm a -

Oh, it would sat - is - fy a fly." "I'm a -

co - zy lit - tle par - lor that would sat - is - fy a fly." "I'm a -

Oh, it would sat - is - fy a fly." "I'm a -

## POSTURE/BREATH

Check your posture and ask yourself these questions.

- Stand with feet apart (Is your weight balanced?)
- Knees unlocked (Can you bend them easily?)
- Back straight (Are you standing erect comfortably and not stiff?)
- Head erect (Is your chin level, and not too far up or down?)
- Rib cage lifted (Is your chest high and able to expand?)
- Shoulders relaxed (Are they comfortably down, not too far forward or back?)
- Hands at your side (Are they relaxed and free of tension?)

### Coordinated Breathing:

When you swing a bat or throw a ball, you use *preparation*, *attack*, and *follow-through*. It's the same with singing:

*Inhalation* - is your preparation. Just like the backswing of the racket, you must judge the distance, length and the loudness of the phrase you will sing.

*Exhalation* - Just like throwing a ball (attack), this is the part of breathing that requires the most coordination. When you throw a ball, your strength, knowledge, technical precision and discipline affect your accuracy. It's the same in breathing. The more you know, the more you've practiced, and the amount of effort you apply all combine to help you sing with a fully supported tone.

*Release* - As you end a musical phrase, follow-through with the breath for a pleasing and accurate release. Just as you wouldn't choke your baseball swing, don't choke off the breath at the end of a phrase. When you release a phrase well, you also prepare for the next breath.

1. Breathe through an imaginary straw. Feel the expansion in your rib cage as your lungs fill with air. Sing the following pattern, and as you release the tone, also exhale the rest of your air. Repeat at different pitch levels.

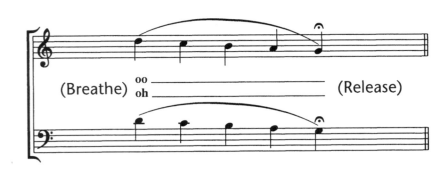

**BREATH**

**The breathing process:** The physical aspect of breathing involves several different parts of the body.

During inhalation, the *diaphragm* muscle contracts, flattens and moves downward toward the feet. This motion pushes against the abdomen, pushing it outward. At the same time, the *intercostal muscles* (rib muscles) also contract, moving the ribs outward, expanding the rib cage. Since the lungs are attached to the diaphragm and the ribs, the lungs expand, and air rushes in.

When you sing, your *exhalation* is controlled, the abdominal muscles contract and the ribs stay expanded to provide resistance and control to the exhalation.

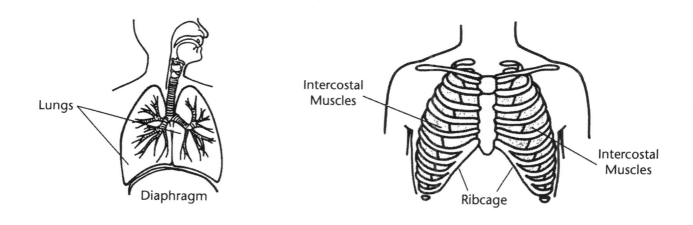

2. As you sing the following exercise, remember to:
- Take a full expanded rib cage breath, remembering "prepare, attack, and follow-through" as you inhale, exhale on a tone, and release.
- Breathe "on the vowel," i.e., if you are to sing an "ah," take your breath in an "ah" shape. This helps prepare you to sing with a relaxed jaw and vertical mouth space.

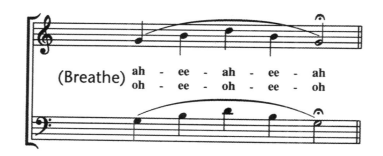

### TRIADS/TONIC CHORD

Let's review chords. In the last chapter we learned that two or more harmonic intervals combined to form a *chord*. So, a *chord* is the combination of three or more tones played or sung simultaneously.

A *triad* is a special type of 3-note chord built in 3rds over a *root tone*. Following are some examples of triads.

When a *triad* is built on the keynote of a major scale it is called a *tonic chord*. You'll notice that the word *tonic* is related to the word tone. *Tonic* is another way of referring to the keynote in a major scale and *tonic chord* is another way of referring to the triad built on that keynote.

### Check your knowledge!

1. How many tones are needed to form a chord?

2. Describe a *triad*.

3. What is another name for keynote?

4. On what tone of the major scale is a tonic chord built?

5. Is the *tonic chord* a triad?

### THE TONIC CHORD

Practice the following drills which use the tonic chord. Remember, when the melody outlines the tonic chord you are singing melodic intervals. When 3 or more parts sing the tonic chord simultaneously, the ensemble is singing a chord.

The Tonic Chord

Tonic Chord Melody Drills

Chord Builders

**TONIC CHORD PRACTICE**

Sing each line separately and in any combination.

## RESTS

*Rests* are silences in music. They come in a variety of lengths, just like notes. These silences are just as important as the notes.

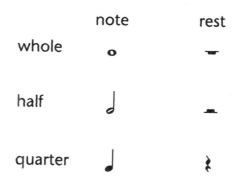

Rests and notes of the same name share the same duration.

## Check your knowledge!

1. Define *rests* in music.

2. Identify the following rests:  𝄽  —  —

3. In $\frac{4}{4}$ meter, how many beats does a whole rest receive? A half rest? A quarter rest?

## PRACTICE WITH RESTS

Read each line (clap, tap, or chant)

**RHYTHM AND PITCH PRACTICE**

Sing each line separately and in any combination.

## MUSICAL TERMS

*Tied notes* - Remember that slurs are curved lines that connect notes of different pitch. Notes are *tied* when a curved line connects notes of the same pitch. When two notes are tied together, their duration equals the combined value of both:

| | | | | | = 5 beats total

*allegro* - originally, this Italian term meant "happy" or "joyful," but now it generally means to perform at a fast tempo.

- a graphic marking meaning *crescendo* (abbr. *cresc.*), gradually louder

- a graphic marking meaning decrescendo (abbr. *descresc.*), gradually softer. The term *diminuendo* (abbr. *dim.*) is also used.

# JUBILATE DEO
### Treble Chorus • Tenor Bass Chorus

*Jubilate Deo* (pronounced *YOO-bee-lah-teh DEH-ahw*) is the Latin text that opens Psalm 100 and may be translated as "be joyful in the Lord." This joyful text lends itself to brilliant musical settings.

As you prepare to perform this piece:
- Read the rhythm of both parts. Notice where you have tied notes and hold those notes for the combined value of both notes.
- Add pitch. Notice where you have melodic skips that outline the intervals in the tonic chord.
- Add the text and repeat as needed for accuracy and to increase the tempo to performance level.
- Sing musically with good tone quality and articulation.

**TREBLE CHORUS**

# Jubilate Deo
For SA a cappella

Music by
JOHN LEAVITT

*Pronounced "Ah-leh-LOO-ee-ah"*

**TENOR BASS CHORUS**

# Jubilate Deo
For TB a cappella

Music by
JOHN LEAVITT

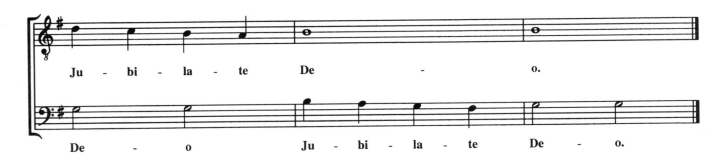

*Pronounced "Ah-leh-LOO-ee-ah"*

## MIXED CHORUS

In the small Massachusetts village where *Emily Dickinson* lived, she was known as an eccentric recluse. After her father's death, she always wore white, and never ventured out of her house. After her own death, her family was astonished to discover that she had written over 1700 poems.  Her work has been praised for its originality and freshness, and she is now recognized as one of America's finest poets.

As you prepare to perform "To Make A Prairie":
- Read the rhythm, noticing where you have tied notes. Hold the tied notes for the combined value of both.
- Add pitch, noticing where the melody outlines the intervals in the tonic chord.
- Sing with good tone, articulation, and expression.

# To Make A Prairie
For SATB a cappella

Poem by
EMILY DICKINSON

Music by
EMILY CROCKER

**REVIEW AND PRACTICE**

In group discussion, answer the following questions, giving examples or illustrating where possible. Refer to **VOICE-BUILDERS** in Chapters 1-6 as needed.

1.  Describe the steps to a good singing posture.

2.  How does good posture affect singing?

3.  How does an expanded rib cage affect breathing?

4.  What is a *yawn-sigh*?

5.  List the *five basic vowels*.

6.  Describe three things you should do to produce the basic mouth position in singing the five basic vowels.

7.  Why do we need *articulation* in singing? What are the *articulators*?

8.  What does the term *breath support* mean?

9.  What is the muscle called that is below the lungs and that moves downward during inhalation?

10. How do the *intercostal muscles* affect the rib cage during breathing?

11. What are the three stages of coordinated breathing?

### Tone/Articulation
Review the elements of good singing in the following exercise:
*   Take a full expanded rib cage breath, and maintain the support while singing the phrase, and release.
*   As you inhale, shape your mouth like the vowel you are preparing to sing.
*   Articulate the underlined consonants.
*   Repeat at different pitch levels, both higher and lower.

**REVIEW AND PRACTICE**

**Check your knowledge!**

1. Name the order of whole/half steps for any major scale.

2. Define *sharp*. Define *flat*.

3. Name two ways sharps and flats can be placed in music.

4. Where is a sharp or flat sign placed in relation to the notehead?

5. Where is a *key signature* placed?

6. Name the key signature for C major. For G major.

7. What is the term for silences in music?

8. Identify the following rests:  ▬  ▬  𝄽

9. In $\frac{4}{4}$ meter, how many quarter rests equal a half rest? In $\frac{4}{4}$ meter, how many half rests equal a whole rest?

10. What is an *interval*?

11. What is the difference between *melodic* and *harmonic* intervals?

12. What is a *chord*?

13. How many tones are needed to form a *chord*?

14. What is the difference between a *chord* and a *triad*?

15. What is another name for *keynote*?

16. On what tone of the major scale is a tonic chord built?

17. Is the tonic chord a triad?

### MUSICAL TERMS

*legato* - indicates that the musical passage is to be played smooth and connected

*sempre* - always; *sempre legato* means "always smooth."

*rit.* - *ritardando*; gradually slowing the tempo.

*poco a poco* - little by little; *poco a poco rit.* means "become slower little by little."

$\bar{\rho}$ - *tenuto accent*; a slight stress of the note and hold the note full value.

## FOND AFFECTION
### Treble Chorus

"Fond Affection" takes its text from a traditional Kentucky folksong.  As you prepare to perform this piece:
- Read the rhythm, noticing rests and tied notes.
- Add the pitch, noticing where the melody outlines the intervals of the tonic chord.  Notice how the parts begin in unison, and then go to a call-response pattern.
- Add the text and accompaniment, and perform with expression.

## THE RAINBOW
### Tenor Bass Chorus

The text of this song is from a poem by *William Wordsworth,* an English poet who lived from 1770-1850. From 1843-1850, Wordsworth served as England's poet laureate, and in that role was responsible for composing poems for royal and national occasions. As you prepare to perform "The Rainbow":
- Read the rhythm, noticing rests and tied notes.
- Add the pitch, noticing where the melody outlines the tonic chord.
- Add the text and accompaniment, and perform expressively.

## HOW DOTH THE LITTLE CROCODILE
### Mixed Chorus

The text of this humorous piece comes from *Alice's Adventures in Wonderland,* by Lewis Carroll (1832-1898), whose real name was Charles Lutwidge Dodgson.
- Read the rhythm, noticing ties and rests.
- Add pitch, noticing where the melody outlines the tonic chord.
- Add the text and accompaniment and perform expressively.

**TREBLE CHORUS**

# Fond Affection
For SA or SSA and Piano

Text: Traditional Kentucky Mountain

Music by
EMILY CROCKER

wade, _____ I'll just go hire a lit-tle boat-man _____

wade, _____ I'll just go hire a lit-tle boat-man _____

wade, _____ I'll just go hire a lit-tle boat-man _____

_____ to row me a-cross the storm-y tide. I give you

_____ to row me a-cross the storm-y tide.

_____ to row me a-cross the storm-y tide.

back _____ your ring and let - ters, al - so the pic - ture

I give you back _____ your ring and let - ters and all that

I give you back _____ your ring and let - ters and all that

I have loved so well, _____ and hence - forth we will meet as

I have loved so well, _____ and hence - forth we will meet, will

I have loved so well, so well, and hence - forth we will meet, will

**TENOR BASS CHORUS**

# The Rainbow

For TB or TTB and Piano

Poem by
WILLIAM WORDSWORTH

Music by
EMILY CROCKER

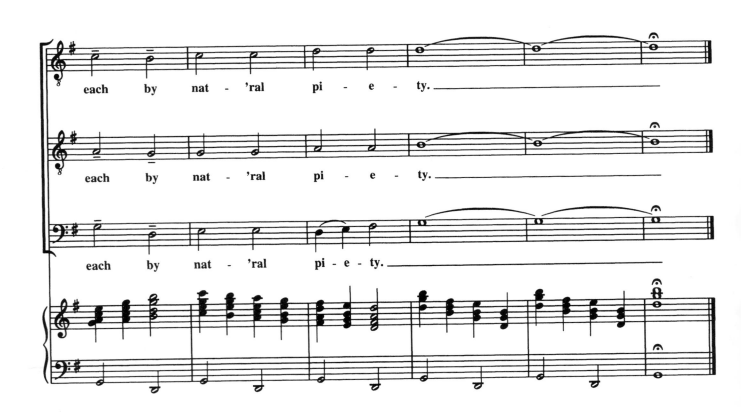

**MIXED CHORUS**

# How Doth The Little Crocodile

(From "Alice's Adventures in Wonderland")
For SATB and Piano

Poem by
**LEWIS CARROLL**

Music by
**JOHN LEAVITT**

## POSTURE/BREATH

1. Stretch high overhead. Bend at the waist and gradually stand upright, one vertebra at a time. Nod your head "yes" several times, then "no."

2. Yawn-sigh.

3. Imagine there is a milkshake as large as the room. "Drink" the air through a large straw. Exhale on a yawn-sigh.

4. Sip in air as though you were sipping water. Notice the cool feeling in your throat.

5. Breathe in with your lips in an "oo" shape, then sing the following exercise. Repeat the pattern at different pitch levels, both higher and lower. Open the vowel to an "ah" as you go higher and an "oh" as you go lower.

(Breathe on "oo") "oo"          (breathe)   *etc.*

6. Take a full, relaxed breath and sing on a staccato "hoo."

Short and detached

hoo    hoo    hoo    hoo    hoo

These exercises, and many others you will learn, contribute toward a relaxed, free, and *open throat*. An open throat will help you produce a free, open tone that is not constricted or tension-filled, and will help keep your voice healthy. This is important as you develop resonance and flexibility in your voice.

**Vocalization:** The source of vocal tone is the *larynx* (pronounced "LEH-rinks" and popularly called the "voice box"). The larynx is a part of the *respiratory system* and is not muscle, but is made of *cartilage*. The larynx is located midway between the mouth, nose and throat above, and the lungs and *trachea* (air passages) below.

You can find your own larynx by locating your "Adam's Apple." If your Adam's apple is not prominent, you can feel it if you lightly run your fingertip down the front of your neck from your chin, until you feel a hard structure with a sharp upper edge. If you hold your finger here while you say "ah" you can feel the vibration that the larynx produces.

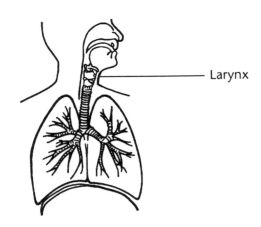

Larynx

### The Vocal Folds

The *vocal folds* (also called *vocal cords*) are a pair of muscles attached to the front and back of the larynx. They open and close somewhat like a valve – open for breathing, closed for singing (and speaking). Exhaled air passes between the gently closed vocal folds, causing them to vibrate. The number of vibrations per second produces pitch. The following illustration shows the vocal folds from above.

The Vocal Folds (seen from above)

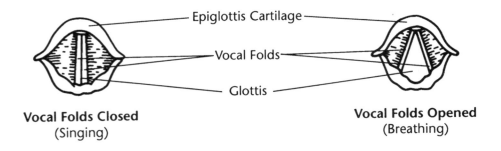

Epiglottis Cartilage

Vocal Folds

Glottis

**Vocal Folds Closed**
(Singing)

**Vocal Folds Opened**
(Breathing)

## MORE ABOUT METER

Remember that *meter* is a form of rhythmic organization. In the simple meters we have been using, the top number indicates the number of beats per measure in the music. The bottom number indicates which note value gets the beat.

4 = Four beats per measure ( ♩ ♩ ♩ ♩ )
4 = The quarter note ( ♩ ) receives the beat

3 = Three beats per measure ( ♩ ♩ ♩ )
4 = The quarter note ( ♩ ) receives the beat

2 = Two beats per measure ( ♩ ♩ )
4 = The quarter note ( ♩ ) receives the beat

So that the ear can easily recognize and group notes into the various meters, each meter stresses certain beats. Almost all meters stress the first beat of each measure. This is called the *downbeat*.

In 4/4 meter, a secondary stress occurs on beat three along with the stressed downbeat.

## Check your knowledge!

1. Define *meter*.

2. Describe the following meters:  3/4   2/4   4/4

3. What is a *downbeat*?

4. What beats are stressed in  4/4  meter? In  3/4  meter? In  2/4  meter?

## METER PRACTICE • DOTTED HALF NOTES

Read the following exercise with changing meters.

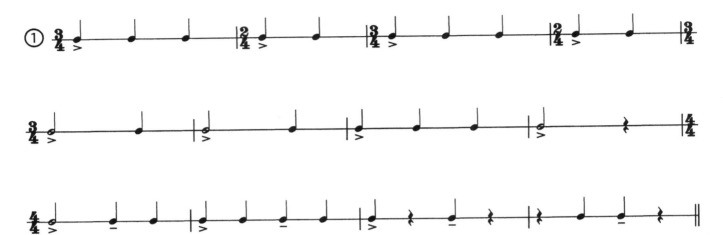

### Dotted half notes

In our music notation, we need to be able to measure note values with durations of three beats (especially in meters of 3). Our notational system accomplishes this by adding a dot to the right of a note head. The rule governing dotted notes is *the dot receives half the value of the note to which it is attached.*

Practice the following exercise in ¾ meter:

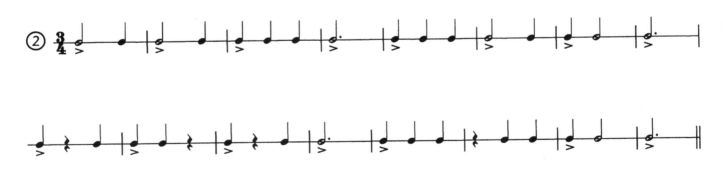

### Check your knowledge!

1. What is the dotted note rule?

2. How many beats does a half note receive in ¾ meter? A dotted half note?

Read each line separately and in any combination.

**UNISON VOICES**

# Three Nursery Rhymes
## I. Humpty Dumpty

For Unison Voices and Piano

Traditional Rhyme

Music by
EMILY CROCKER

Fast (♩ = 132) (♩ = ♩ throughout)

Piano

Humpty Dumpty sat on a wall, Humpty Dumpty

had a great fall; All the King's horses and all the King's

men Could - n't put Hump - ty to - geth - er a - gain!

## II. A Diller, A Dollar

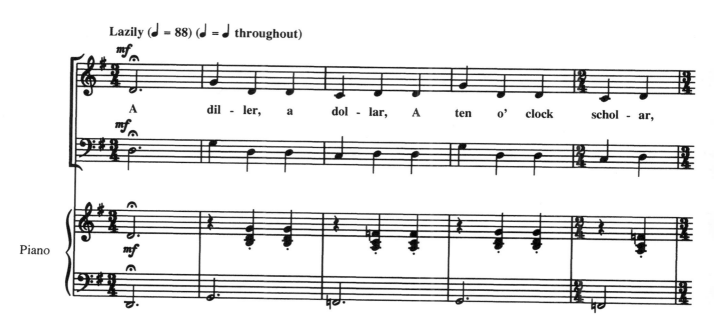

A dil - ler, a dol - lar, A ten o' clock schol - ar,

Piano

What makes you come so soon? You used to come at

ten o' clock, but now you come at noon!

## III. Jack and Jill

**Light and quick (♩ = 132) (♩ = ♩ throughout)**

Piano

### POSTURE/BREATH

1. Stretch overhead, side to side, up and down, then shake to relax any tight muscles.

2. Raise your arms overhead, stretching the fingers out in all directions. Bring the arms back to the sides, relaxed and free of tension.

3. Exhale all your air. Wait for a moment until your body lets you know it needs air. Allow the air to flow in without effort.

4. Sip air through a straw. Allow your lungs and rib cage to expand outward.

5. Place your fingertips just below your rib cage and take a "surprised" breath. Notice the movement of the diaphragm.

### Vowels

Review the 5 basic vowels used in choral singing: ee, eh, ah, oh, oo. Remember when you sing these vowels to sing with a relaxed jaw and vertical space inside the mouth.

## Vowels

There are many other vowel sounds used in both speaking and singing. Here are some examples of other vowel sounds. As a general rule: Sing the vowel sound as you would say it, but modify the vowel in the following ways:

- Keep a relaxed jaw
- Maintain vertical space inside the mouth
- Keep the corners of the mouth from spreading outward
- Repeat at different pitch levels

⑦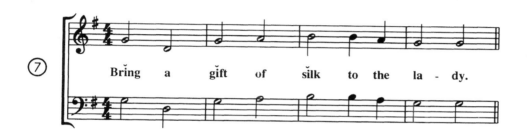

Bring a gift of silk to the la - dy.

" ĭ " as in <u>gift</u>

⑧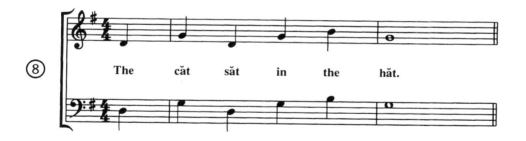

The căt săt in the hăt.

" ă " as in <u>cat</u>

⑨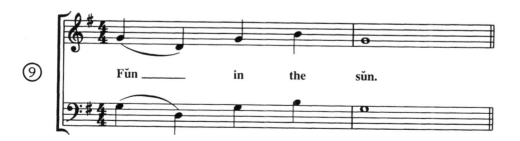

Fŭn _____ in the sŭn.

" ŭ " as in <u>fun</u>

## EIGHTH NOTES AND RESTS

So far, we've used whole, half, and quarter notes. An *eighth note* ( ♪ ) is half the value of a quarter note. Two eighth notes ( ♫ ) have the same duration as one quarter note. The eighth note has a corresponding rest, the *eighth rest* ( ʼ ) which shares the same length as an eighth note.

Below is a chart summarizing the notes and rests we've learned.

|         | note | rest |
|---------|------|------|
| whole   | o    | ▬    |
| half    | ♩    | ▬    |
| quarter | ♩    | 𝄽    |
| eighth  | ♪    | ʼ    |

The following diagram summarizes the relationships between the notes we've studied:

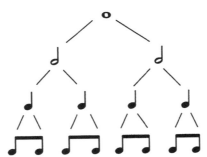

## More about eighth notes

If the quarter note receives the beat, you can consider eighth notes to be a division of the beat:

beat:

division:

Eighth notes may be notated singly with a stem and a flag:

Or they may be beamed together in groups:

## Check your knowledge!

1. How many eighth notes equal a quarter note? A half note? A whole note?

2. Describe two ways eighth notes can be notated.

**RHYTHM PRACTICE**

Read each line (clap, tap, or chant).

**SPEECH CHORUS**

# The Kangaroo

For 2-Part Speech Chorus

Music by
JOHN LEAVITT

 **POSTURE/BREATH**

1. Stretch your arms overhead, then bend at the waist and stretch toward the floor. Slowly rise up, one vertebra at a time until you are in a standing posture.

2. Rotate your shoulders, first your left, then your right, then both shoulders. Raise your head so that it is in line with the spinal column, and not tilted up or down. Remember to stand in a good singing posture:
   • Stand with feet apart (Is your weight balanced?)
   • Knees unlocked (Can you bend them easily?)
   • Back straight (Are you standing erect comfortably and not stiff?)
   • Head erect (Is your chin level, and not too far up or down?)
   • Rib cage lifted (Is your chest high and able to expand?)
   • Shoulders relaxed (Are they comfortably down, not too far forward or back?)
   • Hands at your side (Are they relaxed and free of tension?)

3. When people are suddenly startled, they usually take a deep natural breath very quickly. Take a "surprised" breath. Notice the action of the *diaphragm*.

4. Imagine that there is an elevator platform at the bottom of your lungs. Drop the platform toward the floor as you inhale. Inhale 4 counts, exhale 4 counts. Repeat with 5, then 6 counts.

**Physical Exercise:** A regular program of physical exercise is very useful in the development of a singer. Exercise improves breath capacity, the cardiovascular system, endurance, and general good health. Be sure to have a physician's approval before beginning any exercise program, but the benefits of such a program are significant.

**Tone/Articulation**
Review the following vowels: ĭ (gift), ă (cat), ŭ (run)

### THE NEUTRAL VOWEL

The second syllable of the following words and several one-syllable words use what is called the *neutral vowel*, also called *schwa* (ə). It might be described as similar to an "uh" sound, and is usually an unstressed word or syllable. To produce this vowel:

- Keep space inside the mouth.
- Maintain a vertical mouth shape.
- Do not allow the corners of the mouth to spread outward.
- The mouth is more closed than an "ah" vowel.

Examples:

| (ə) | (ə) | (ə) | (ə) | (ə) | (ə) | (ə) | (ə) |
|-----|-----|-----|-----|-----|-----|-----|-----|
| <u>so</u>fa | n<u>ea</u>rest | q<u>ui</u>et | <u>au</u>tumn | jo<u>y</u>ous | <u>of</u> | <u>the</u> | w<u>ou</u>ldn't |

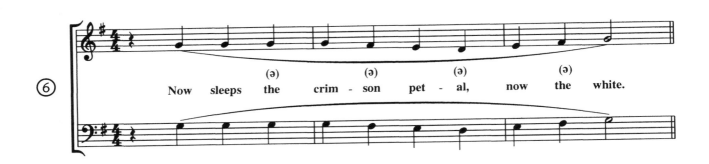

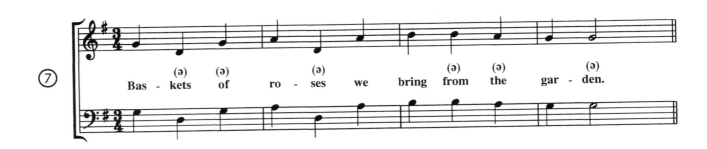

### THE DOMINANT CHORD

Let's review chords. So far we've learned that two or more harmonic intervals form a chord. So, a chord is the combination of three or more tones played or sung simultaneously.

Remember that a triad is a special type of 3-note chord built in 3rds over a root tone. Following are some examples of triads.

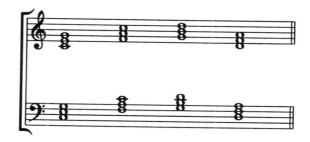

When a triad is built on the key note or 1st degree of a major scale, it is called a *tonic* chord. In tonal music, pitches and chords have relationships with each other. Some pitches and chords create a sense of resolution (at ease, rest) while others create a sense of momentum (movement or energy). The tonic chord creates a sense of resolution.

The *dominant* chord is a triad built on the 5th degree of a major scale. The dominant chord is perhaps the strongest chord of momentum, generally wanting to return home to the tonic.

G Major

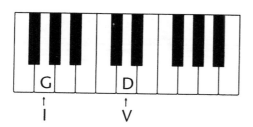

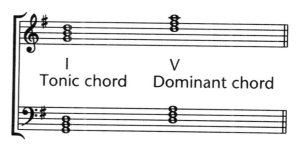

### Check your knowledge!

1. On which degree of the major scale is the dominant chord built? The tonic chord?

2. Which chord creates a sense of resolution? Which chord creates a sense of momentum?

**CHORD DRILLS**

**CHORD DRILLS**

Chord Drills

I (Tonic)          V (Dominant)          V (Dominant)          I (Tonic)

# Skip To My Lou

For SA, TB or SATB a cappella

Traditional Game Song

Soprano: Skip,   skip,   skip   to my Lou,      skip,   skip,   skip   to my Lou,

Alto: Skip, skip,  skip,    skip   to my Lou,  skip, skip, skip,    skip   to my

Tenor: Skip, skip,  skip,    skip   to my Lou,  skip, skip, skip,    skip   to my

Bass: Skip,   skip,   skip   to my Lou,      skip,   skip,   skip   to my Lou,

skip,   skip,   skip   to my Lou,      skip   to my Lou, my   dar - ling.

Lou,   skip, skip,  skip,    skip   to my Lou,      my ___ dar - ling.

Lou,   skip, skip,  skip,    skip   to my Lou,      my ___ dar - ling.

skip,   skip,   skip   to my Lou,      skip   to my Lou, my   dar - ling.

**TREBLE CHORUS**

# Long, Long Ago

For SSA a cappella

By THOMAS BAYLY

Arranged by
JOHN LEAVITT

**TENOR BASS CHORUS**

# Down In The Valley
For TTB a cappella

American Folksong

Arranged by
JOHN LEAVITT

**MIXED CHORUS**

# The Three Rogues

For SATB a cappella

Traditional English

Arranged by
EMILY CROCKER

## REVIEW AND PRACTICE

1. Describe the steps for a good singing posture.

2. How does an expanded rib cage affect breath capacity?

3. What are the five basic vowel sounds? Describe formation of these vowels.

4. What is the general rule for producing other vowel sounds in addition to the five basic vowel sounds?

5. What is the *neutral vowel*?

6. Describe the difference in the vowel sounds of the following:
   • 2nd syllable of *sofa*
   • 1st syllable of *father*

7. What is *articulation* in singing?  What are the three main *articulators*?

8. What is the source of vocal tone?  What is it popularly called?

9. How do the vocal folds produce sound?

10. How can physical exercise help to improve singing?

### Tone/Articulation
Review all the elements of good singing in the following exercise, especially vertical vowel shape and articulation.

Text by William Shakespeare

In sweet mu - sic is such art kill - ing care and grief of heart.

**REVIEW AND PRACTICE**

**Check your knowledge!**

1.  What is the dotted note rule?

2.  How many beats does a half note receive in $\frac{3}{4}$ meter?  A dotted half note?

3.  How many eighth notes equal a quarter note?  A half note?  A whole note?

4.  Describe two ways eighth notes can be notated.

5.  Define meter.

6.  Describe the following meters: $\frac{4}{4}$, $\frac{3}{4}$, $\frac{2}{4}$ .

7.  What is a downbeat?

8.  What beats are stressed in $\frac{4}{4}$ meter?  In $\frac{3}{4}$ meter?  In $\frac{2}{4}$ meter?

9.  On what degree of a major scale is a dominant chord built?  Spell a dominant chord in the following keys:  C and G major.

10.  Give a description of the relationship between tonic and dominant chords.

Matching Drill

①  a) downbeat

②  b) dotted half note

③  c) dominant in G major

④  d) tonic in C major

⑤  e) dominant in C major

⑥  f) tonic in G major

**TREBLE CHORUS**

# He Is Born
For SSA and Piano

French Carol

Arranged by
EMILY CROCKER

* Opt. 8va through measure 17
if range is too low.

**TENOR BASS CHORUS**

# Sweet Betsy From Pike

For TB or TTB and Piano

Traditional Folksong

Arranged by
EMILY CROCKER

old  yel - low   dog. }
won - der - f'lly  sad. }   Sing-ing  too - ra - loo - ra - too - ra - lee -

ay,   Sing - ing  too - ra - loo - ra - too - ra - lee -

**MIXED CHORUS**

# Hush, Little Baby

For SATB and Piano

Traditional

Arranged by
JOHN LEAVITT

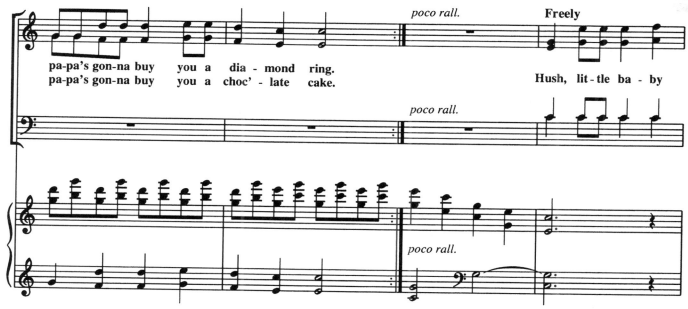

pa-pa's gon-na buy you a dia - mond ring.
pa-pa's gon-na buy you a choc' - late cake.

*poco rall.*  **Freely**

Hush, lit - tle ba - by

don't you cry, ma-ma's gon-na sing you a lull - a - bye._____

Mm

## POSTURE/BREATH

1. Lift the left shoulder high and then let it fall. Repeat with the right shoulder and then both shoulders. Drop the head gently to the chest and then let it roll to the right and then to the left. Stretch overhead, fall forward like a rag doll and then gradually stand up to a good singing posture.

2. Breathe in from the waist. Imagine you are able to draw in air from four separate openings in your waist – front, back, side, and side. Inhale over 4 counts, exhale on "ss" over 4 counts. Repeat with 6, then 8 counts.

### Registers

The singing voice can be divided into three basic regions, called registers. These registers are often identified as *chest* (low), *middle*, and *head* (high) registers. By working consistently on the breath, forming correct vowels, and producing a good tone, a singer can unify these registers to produce a smooth, natural-sounding voice.

3. "The Roller Coaster" – Imitate the movement of a roller coaster with your voice as it soars up and down and loops the loop. Sing on an "oo" vowel, an "oh" vowel, and on "m," "n," or "ng" consonant sounds.

4. Yawn-sigh.

5. Sing the following exercise. Repeat at different pitch levels:

**The Male Changing Voice:** As the male voice matures, it changes in both pitch and timbre (tone quality). This presents challenges to the singer as he participates in choral groups. There may be certain pitches that at one time were easy to sing, that suddenly are out of range. Fortunately, with practice, and attention to the principles of good singing, a male singer can negotiate this period with relatively little difficulty.

**Falsetto:** This term comes from the Latin word *falsus,* meaning "false." This voice is a fourth register in the male voice that extends far above the natural high voice.

Through breath support and resonance, singing in the falsetto voice can help the male singer develop the middle and head registers. For male singers whose voices have changed, this register is literally in the same pitch range as the treble voice.

Experiment with the falsetto voice in the following exercises. (Note: Treble voices sing these exercises in head register)

6.  Repeat the yawn-sigh and roller coaster exercises on page 110, but make sure that all male voices are singing in the treble (falsetto) register.

7.  Sing the following exercise, with changing or changed voices in falsetto and treble voices in head voice:

For a time, the "new baritone" voice may find it difficult to sing the notes around middle C. While these notes may seem "high," it is important to recognize that tenor, baritone, and even bass voices often perform music which uses these pitches. As you practice falsetto exercises which move in a downward direction, work consistently in the area around middle C. This will help develop the male middle and head registers, and smooth out these levels or "breaks" in the voice.

8.  Practice this exercise, repeating it a half step lower each time. Male voices should begin in falsetto, changing into head, middle, and finally chest register. Modify the vowel (oo, oh, ah, aw) as needed.

9.  Yawn-sigh.

## TONE

In the following exercise, concentrate on the following:
- Maintain good intonation as you outline the I and V chords.
- Change registers smoothly as you change from the "oo" to the "oh" vowels.
- Produce the "L" consonant using the tip of the tongue.

In the following exercise, concentrate on the following:
- Good intonation on a descending scale pattern
- Expanded rib cage breathing
- Smooth melodic line

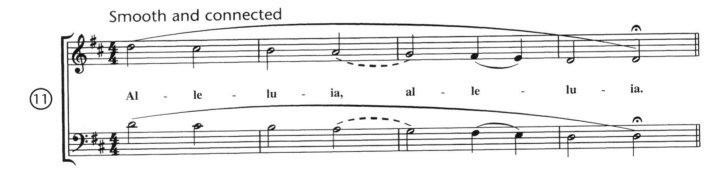

In the following exercise, concentrate on the following:
- Activate the diaphragm for staccato articulation
- Change registers smoothly as you change from the "eh" to the "oo" vowel ("hey you")

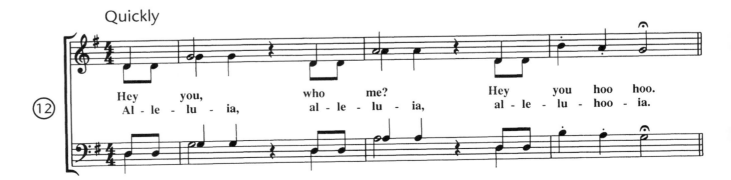

## KEY OF F MAJOR

The key of F major indicates that the key note will be F. The graphic below shows the F major scale as well as the whole/half step progression that is required for a major scale.

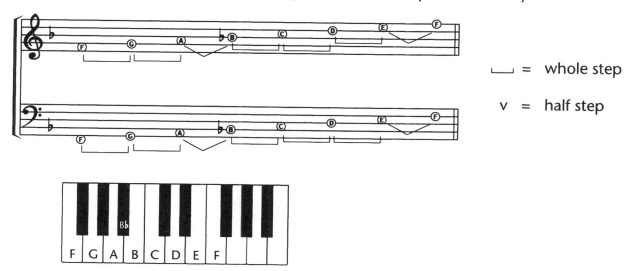

⌐⌐ = whole step

v = half step

This time, the whole/half step progression requires a B flat. If we had written A-B, the interval between these two pitches would have been a whole step rather than the required half step.

Remember that a key signature is placed after the clef sign at the beginning of a line. This time the flat is on B's line, and indicates that every time B occurs in the music, it should be sung as a B flat.

### Key Relationships

So far, we've studied three keys: C, G, and F. C major has no sharps or flats. G major has one sharp, F♯, and F major has one flat, B♭. G major and F major are considered neighboring keys to C major because the differences in the key signatures is only one note. Notice that G major (a sharp key) lies an interval of a fifth *higher* than C, and F major, (a flat key) lies an interval of a fifth *lower* than C.

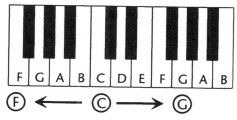

### Check your knowledge!

1. What is the key signature for F major? For G major? For C major?

2. What is the interval that relates C major to F and G?

**KEY OF F CHORD DRILLS**

## RHYTHM AND PITCH PRACTICE

Sing each line separately and in any combination.

**TREBLE** • **TENOR BASS** • **MIXED**

# Hosanna In Excelsis Deo

For 2, 3 or 4-part Canon a cappella

Adapted from
**WOLFGANG MOZART**

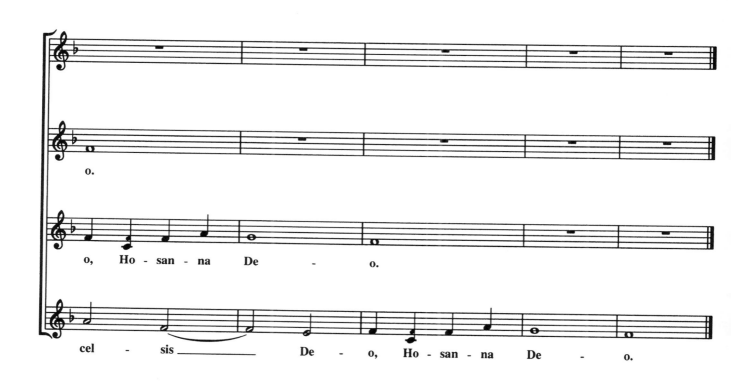

## POSTURE/BREATH

1. Stand in your best singing posture.  Imagine there is a balloon attached to the top of your head.  Allow the balloon to bring your head into alignment with your spine.

2. Exhale your air on a "ss" like air escaping from a tire. On a signal from your director, stop the air, and notice the breath support from the diaphragm.

3. Imagine that as you inhale you are filling a balloon with air.  Inhale over 8 counts, exhale on a "ss."

## ARTICULATION

In our daily speech we are often careless about pronouncing all the sounds of all the words:

*I gotta go home now.  Are ya goin' t' the dance?   Who ya goin' with?*

In choral singing, however, it's important to articulate the diction clearly, otherwise the performance will sound ragged and sloppy.  Here are a few exercises to practice articulation. Speak each phrase first, then sing it on a repeated unison pitch or scale pattern.

### "t" and "d"

Both consonants are produced with the tip of the tongue, but "t" is "unvoiced" and "d" is voiced. Notice that sometimes the "t" sound is used even when there is no "t" in the word: *laughed* is pronounced *laft*.

4. Repeat the following "t" patterns:
   - t  t  t  t  t  t  t  t
   - *Tiptoe through the tulips*
   - *Two times ten is twenty*
   - *He laughed.  She talked.  We worked.  They hoped.*

5. Repeat the following:
   - d  d  d  d  d  d  d
   - *day by day*
   - *dream a dream*
   - *do or die*

### ARTICULATION

#### "t" and "d" before a vowel
When "t" or "d" is followed by a syllable or word beginning with a vowel, connect the "t" with that vowel:

- *What a surprise!*
- *Wait until tomorrow.*
- *Sweet is the sound.*
- *The winding road*
- *Open the window*
- *Ride off into the sunset*

#### "t" and "d" before a consonant
Even though in speaking, we often drop a "t" or "d" before a consonant, singing it that way would sound careless. Practice these consonant sounds, followed by the same sound on a short phrase:

- *t-b, t-b, t-b*      *might belong, might belong*
- *t-d, t-d, t-d*      *sweet dessert, sweet dessert*
- *t-f, t-f, t-f*      *Is it free? Is it free?*
- *d-m, d-m, d-m*      *We could meet you there.*
- *d-th, d-th, d-th*      *Sound the trumpet*

#### "t" followed by another "t" – "d" followed by another "d"
Most of the time when a "t" or "d" is followed by another "t" or "d," you will want to pronounce only one of them.

- *I went to see the doctor.*
- *Come at ten o'clock.*
- *We had a great time.*
- *Pretty as a picture*
- *Written on the wall*
- *Hey diddle diddle, the cat and the fiddle*

#### "t" followed by an "s"
Most of the time, you will want to connect the "t" with the "s."

- *sweet song*
- *great sound*
- *street sign*
- *Mozart sonata*
- *short story*

## SUBDOMINANT CHORD

Let's review the chords we've learned so far. The *tonic* chord is a triad built on the key tone or 1st degree of a major scale. The *dominant* chord is a triad built on the 5th degree of a major scale.

The *subdominant* chord is a triad built on the fourth degree of a major scale.

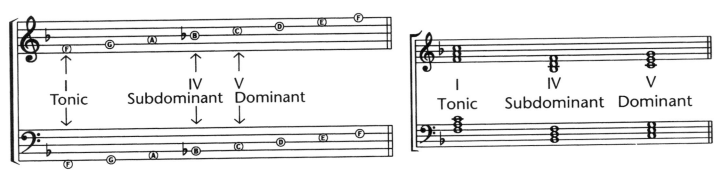

We've discussed the relationship of the tonic and dominant chords. In adding the subdominant chord, here is a description of the chords.

*Tonic* - at rest, at ease, home

*Subdominant* - digression or departure (away from the tonic)

*Dominant* - energy, momentum or movement (toward the tonic)

NOTE: The subdominant degree of the scale and the subdominant chord borrow their name from the dominant. If the dominant lies a fifth higher than the tonic, the *sub*dominant lies a fifth lower than the tonic.

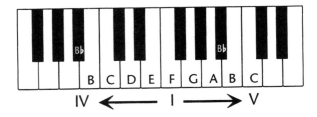

## Check your knowledge!
1. On what degree of a major scale is the subdominant chord built?

2. Describe the tonic, subdominant, and dominant chords. Spell these three chords in C, F, and G major.

3. From where does the subdominant chord borrow its name?

**CHORD DRILLS**

SATB Chord Builders

SSA Chord Builders

TTB Chord Builders

*The vi chord is described in the appendix.*

**RHYTHM AND PITCH PRACTICE**

Read each line separately and in any combination.

**TREBLE • TENOR BASS • MIXED**

# SAN SERINÍ
### Treble Chorus • Tenor Bass Chorus

**Music History:** This simple children's song is from Puerto Rico. The words describe life in a place called San Seriní. As they sing, the children perform the movement of the workers they name: the *zapateros* (shoemakers) and *carpinteros* (carpenters).

**Pronunciation Guide:**

*San Seriní. de la buena vida.*
Sahn Seh-ree-NEE, deh lah BWEH-nah VEE-dah.

*Hacen así, hacen los zapateros (carpinteros)*
Ah-sehn ah-SEE, Ah-sehn lohs zah-pah-TEH-rohs
(kahr-peen-TEH-rohs)

*Así me gusta a mí.*
ah-SEE meh GOOS-tah ah mee.

As you prepare to perform *San Seriní*:
- Read the rhythm, and speak the pitch names in rhythm.
- Sing the pitches. Notice the places where you have intervals of the tonic, subdominant, and dominant chords.
- Practice the Spanish text in rhythm, remembering to sing with tall vowels and good articulation. Wherever you have an "r", "roll" or "trill" the "r" sound, as this is a charactistic of good Spanish pronunciation.
- Sing with the text. Repeat as needed for accuracy, and to increase the tempo to performance level.
- Sing musically with good tone quality and articulation.

# SET ME AS A SEAL
### Mixed Chorus

This contemporary setting of a Biblical text from the *Song of Solomon* makes use of a technique called *suspension*. In measure 10, the soprano, tenor, and bass form a tonic chord in the key of F major. The alto, however, continues to sing the G that was "suspended" from the previous measure. On the third beat of the measure, the alto moves down ("resolves") to an F. The *suspension* produces a sense of tension, or *dissonance*, and the *resolution* produces a sense of repose, or *consonance*.

Suspension Resolution

**TREBLE CHORUS**

# San Seriní
For SSA a cappella

Hispanic Children's Song

Arranged by
EMILY CROCKER

**TENOR BASS CHORUS**

# San Seriní
### For TTB a cappella

**Hispanic Children's Song**

Arranged by
**EMILY CROCKER**

**MIXED CHORUS**

# Set Me As A Seal

For SATB and Piano

Song of Soloman 8: 6-7

Music by
JOHN LEAVITT

## POSTURE/BREATH

1.  Stretch your arms overhead, then bend at the waist and stretch toward the floor. Slowly rise up, one vertebra at a time until you are in a standing posture.

2.  Rotate your shoulders, first your left, then your right, then both shoulders. Raise your head so that it is in line with the spinal column, and not tilted up or down. Stand in a good singing posture:
    *   Stand with feet apart
    *   Knees unlocked
    *   Back straight
    *   Head erect
    *   Rib cage lifted
    *   Shoulders relaxed
    *   Hands at your side

### Resonance

In the following exercise, sing the word "sing" and immediately close to the "ng" sound. You will notice that the sound is very nasal and small. On cue from your director, open the "ng" to an "ah" and notice what happens in your mouth. Did you feel your throat "opening" into a fuller sound? This movement is called "raising the *soft palate*," and helps give the voice *resonance*.

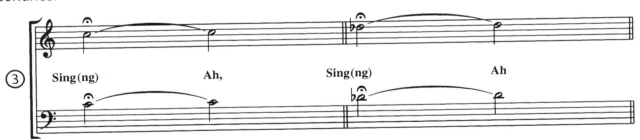

The *soft palate* is located at the back of the roof of the mouth. It is the soft, fleshy part directly behind the hard palate.

*Resonance* comes from the Latin word *resonare* which means to resound. In singing, the sound which comes from the vibrating vocal cords is not audible until it is *amplified* (made louder) by coming into contact with the bony regions of the body and face. This amplification develops and increases the sound.

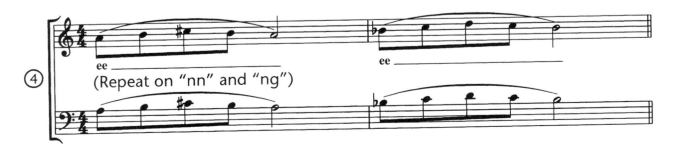

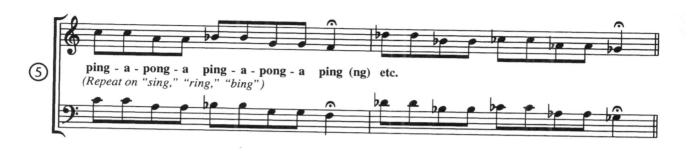

⑤ ping - a - pong - a   ping - a - pong - a   ping (ng) etc.
*(Repeat on "sing," "ring," "bing")*

By slightly changing the position of your jaw, tongue, lips and soft palate, as you produce different vowel sounds, you can increase the resonance in your voice, and enjoy a fuller, ringing sound, as well as reduce voice strain and breathiness in the tone.

⑥ zee _____ oh   oh _____ ee   zee _____ oh   oh _____ ee

## Articulation

Remember the articulators we use to produce clear diction: lips, teeth, and tongue. The movements of these three articulators and other parts of the vocal tract affect the quality and sound of your voice.

Sing the following exercise in unison and in a round with up to five parts. Repeat at different pitch levels.

⑦ *Group I*
Zing-a-zing-a-zee,   zing-a-zing-a-zee,   zing-a-zing-a-zing-a-zing-a-zee.   *Group II* Bla-bla-bla   bla-bla-bla

*Group III*
bla-bla-bla-bla-bla   Yoh   yoh   yah   yah   yoh   yoh   yah   *Group IV* Hoo hoo hoo hoo hoo hoo hoo hoo

*Group V*
hoo   hoo   hoo   hoo   hoo   Bim bom bim(m) bim bom bim(m)   bim bom(m) bim bom bim bom

## KEY OF D MAJOR

The key of D major indicates that the key note will be D. The graphic below shows the D major scale as well as the whole/half step progression that is required for a major scale.

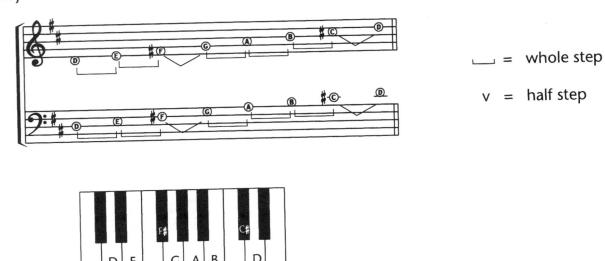

⌐⌐ = whole step

∨ = half step

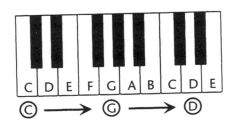

The whole/half step progression this time requires an F♯ and a C♯. If we had written F - G and C-D, the interval between these sets of pitches would have been a whole step rather than the required half step. Thus the key signature for D major is F♯ and C♯ (in that order).

Remember that G major with one sharp (F♯) lies an interval of a fifth higher than C major (which has no sharps or flats). D major, which has two sharps, lies a fifth higher than G major.

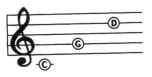

## Check your knowledge!

1. What is the key signature for D major? For G major? For C major?

2. Name where the half steps occur in the D major scale.

## CHORD DRILLS · MELODIC PATTERNS

**SATB Chord Builders**

**SSA Chord Builders**

**TTB Chord Builders**

## MELODY DRILLS

Read each line separately and in any combination.

**TREBLE CHORUS**

# The Flowers
For SA and Piano

Words by
ROBERT LOUIS STEVENSON (1850-1894)

Music by
JOHN LEAVITT

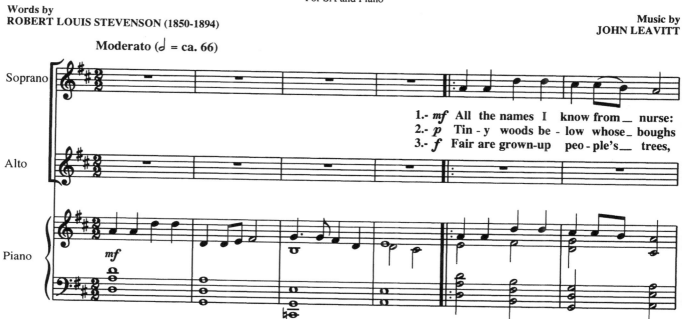

And the La - dy ___ Hol - ly - hock.
Where the brav - er ___ fair - ies climb!
I should live for ___ good and all!

And the La - dy  Hol - ly - hock.
Where the brav - er  fair - ies climb!
I should live for  good and all!

**TENOR BASS CHORUS**

# Sing Me A Song Of A Lad That Is Gone

For TB and Piano

Words by
**ROBERT LOUIS STEVENSON (1850-1894)**

Music by
**JOHN LEAVITT**

With spirit! ($\downarrow$ = ca. 84)

Sing me a song of a

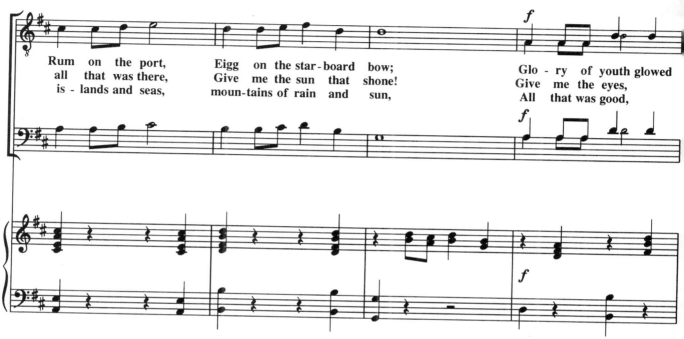

Rum on the port, Eigg on the star-board bow;
all that was there, Give me the sun that shone!
is - lands and seas, moun-tains of rain and sun,

*f*

Glo - ry of youth glowed
Give me the eyes,
All that was good,

in his soul: Where is that glo - ry now?
Give me the soul, Give me the lad _ that's gone.
All that was fair, All that was me _ is

*sub. p*

1,2

gone.

All that was me is gone! Hey!

# See Them Dance

(Les Petites Marionettes)

For SATB a cappella

**French Game Song**

Arranged by
**EMILY CROCKER**

140

 **POSTURE/BREATH**

1. Stretch, then yawn-sigh.

2. Stand in your best singing posture. Imagine that your head is attached by a string to a balloon. The balloon floats upward, bringing your head and body into alignment.

3. Sniff in air in 4 short sniffs quickly, exhale on 4 short puffs. Repeat with 5, then 6. Yawn-sigh.

4. Raise your arms to the sides and overhead while inhaling. Pause for a moment to feel your expanded rib cage. Exhale on a "ss" while slowly lowering your arms.

5. Raise your arms while inhaling as in #4, but as you lower your arms sing a phrase of a song with long phrases, such as "America" or "The Ash Grove":

(Long slow breath while raising arms overhead; lower arms as you sing.)
*My country, 'tis of thee, sweet land of liberty, of thee I sing.*

(Long slow breath while raising arms overhead; lower arms as you sing.)
*Land where my fathers died, land of the pilgrims' pride,*

(Long slow breath while raising arms overhead; lower arms as you sing.)
*From ev'ry mountainside, let freedom ring.*

## Activating the diaphragm

Activating the diaphragm can help to produce staccato, accents and more understandable consonants in choral singing. Do the following exercises and concentrate on the movement of the diaphragm.

6. Place your fingertips just below your rib cage and just above your belt and concentrate on moving the diaphragm as you whisper the following consonant patterns:

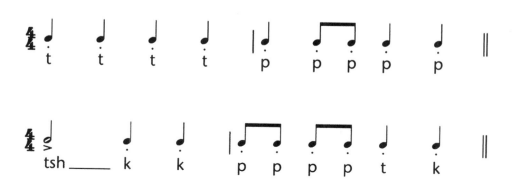

7. In the following exercise, use diaphragm activity to produce the articulation. Try the exercise first on "hoo," then on "oo" with diaphragm activity only, not by using the throat.

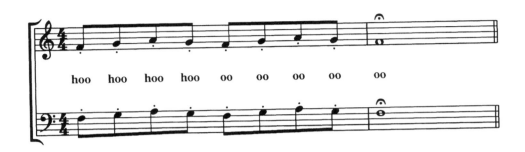

hoo   hoo   hoo   hoo   oo   oo   oo   oo   oo

**Tone/Resonance**
The following exercises help to develop resonance. As you practice, concentrate on feeling the vibration in the face and nasal area.

8. Yawn, then sigh from a high pitch on a "hm."

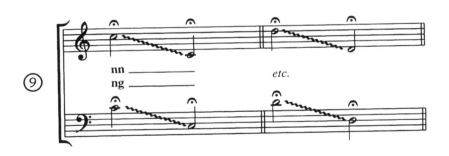

⑨   nn _____   ng _____   *etc.*

⑩   mm _____   nn _____   ng _____

## NASAL TONE

While practicing "m," "n," and "ng" can help a singer discover his/her natural resonance, sometimes these nasal consonants can create a nasal effect on the vowels that surround them. While this nasality is a characteristic of the speech of many Americans, the goal of a pleasing choral tone quality requires that this nasality be corrected, at least while singing. As a singer, it is important to learn techniques that affect and control your own tone quality.

Nasality occurs most often on the following vowels:

|     |                 |
|-----|-----------------|
| ă   | (as in "and")   |
| ow  | (as in "down")  |
| ī   | (as in "time")  |
| ā   | (as in "came")  |
| ĭ   | (as in "sing")  |

In order to correct nasality, it's important to treat the "m," "ng," or "n" like any other consonant.

* For the "m," bring the lips together after the vowel.

  ti → → me
* For the "n," raise the tip of the tongue after the vowel.

  a → → nd
* For the "ng," the tip of the tongue stays down, while the middle of the tongue raises to the hard palate after the vowel.

  si → → ng

Practice the following exercises to help avoid nasality:

## SIXTEENTH NOTES AND RESTS

So far we've used whole, half, quarter and eighth notes. A sixteenth note ( ♪ ) is half the value of an eighth note. Two sixteenth notes ( ♫ ) have the same duration as one eighth note. The sixteenth note has a corresponding rest, the sixteenth rest ( ♦ ) which shares the same length as a sixteenth note.

This chart summarizes the notes and rests we've learned.

|  | note | rest |
|---|---|---|
| whole | o | — |
| half | ♩ | ▬ |
| quarter | ♩ | 𝄽 |
| eighth | ♪ | 𝄾 |
| sixteenth | ♬ | 𝄿 |

The following diagram summarizes the relationships between the notes we've studied:

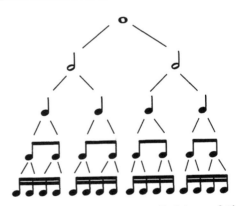

### More about sixteenth notes

If the quarter note receives the beat, you can consider eighth notes to be a *division* of the beat, and sixteenth notes to be a *subdivision* of the beat.

beat:

division:

subdivision:

Sixteenth notes may be notated singly with a stem and a flag:

Or they may be beamed together in groups:

### Check your knowledge!

1. How many sixteenth notes equal an eighth note? A quarter note? A half note? A whole note?

2. Describe two ways sixteenth notes can be notated.

**SIXTEENTH NOTES AND RESTS**

Read each line. (Clap, tap, or chant).

**SPEECH CHORUS**

# Intery Mintery

For 2-Part Speech Chorus

Traditional Counting-out Rhyme

Arranged by
EMILY CROCKER

**SPEECH CHORUS**

# The Jumblies
### For 2-Part Speech Chorus

Words by
**EDWARD LEAR (1812-1888)**

Music by
**JOHN LEAVITT**

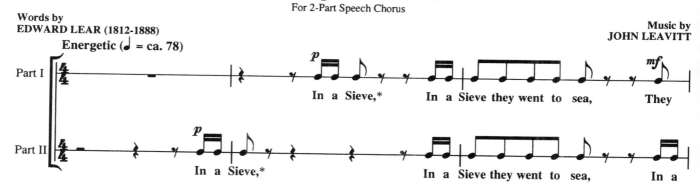

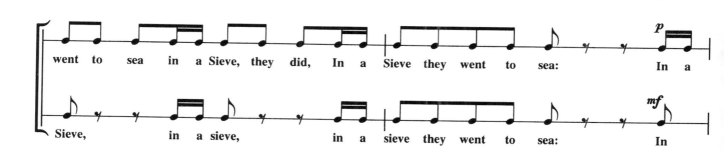

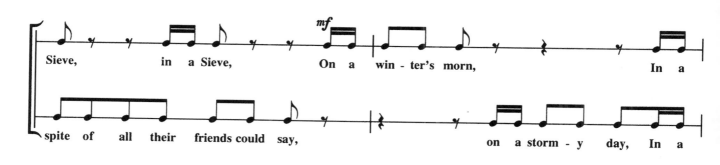

*Pronounced "sihv"

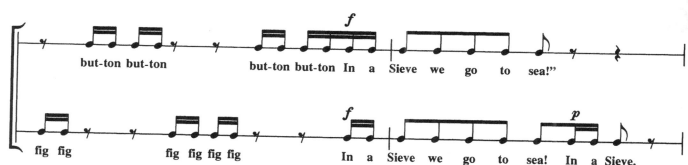

but-ton but-ton     but-ton but-ton In a Sieve we go to sea!"

fig fig     fig fig fig fig     In a Sieve we go to sea! In a Sieve,

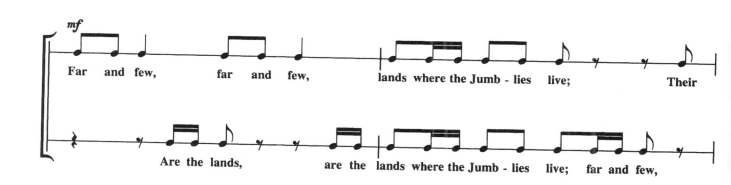

Far and few,     far and few,     lands where the Jumb - lies live;     Their

Are the lands,     are the lands where the Jumb - lies live; far and few,

heads are green,     And they went to sea in a Sieve.     In a

and their hands are blue, And they went to sea in a Sieve.

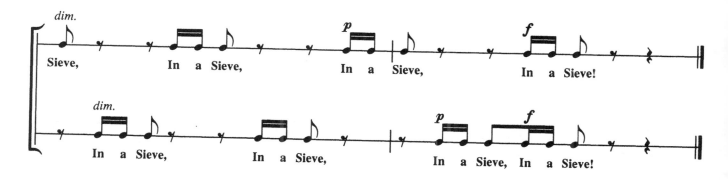

Sieve,     In a Sieve,     In a Sieve,     In a Sieve!

In a Sieve,     In a Sieve,     In a Sieve, In a Sieve!

### REVIEW AND PRACTICE

1. What are the three registers of the singing voice?

2. What is *falsetto*?

3. Demonstrate or describe the pronounciation of "t" and "d" in the following phrases:
   *Sweet is the sound*
   *Sound the trumpet*
   *Great day!*

4. What is *resonance* in singing?

5. How does the *soft palate* affect resonance?

6. Describe techniques to prevent a nasal tone quality.

### Tone/Resonance/Articulation

Review the elements of good singing as you practice the following exercises:

## REVIEW

### Check your knowledge!

1. Name the key signature for the following major keys:  C, G, D, F.

2. On which degree of the major scale is the tonic chord built?

3. On which degree of the major scale is the subdominant chord built?

4. On which degree of the major scale is the dominant chord built?

5. Describe the relationship of the tonic, subdominant, and dominant chords.  Spell these three chords in C, G, D, and F major.

6. From where does the subdominant chord borrow its name?

7. How many sixteenth notes equal an eighth note?  A quarter note?  A half note?  A whole note?

8. In $\frac{4}{4}$ meter, which note value represents the beat?  The division?  The subdivision?

### Matching Drill

①

②

③

④

⑤

⑥

⑦

a)  division of beat

b)  beat

c)  dominant in G major

d)  subdominant in C major

e)  subdivision of beat

f)  tonic in D major

g)  dominant in F major

**MELODY DRILLS**

Sing each line separately and in any combination.

**TREBLE CHORUS**

# All Join Hands

For SSA a cappella

Game Song, adapted

Arranged by
EMILY CROCKER

Round and a-round and a-round we go; Round and a-round and a-round we go;

Round and round we go; round and round we go;

Round and a-round and a-round and a-round and a-round and a-round and a-round and round we

Round and a-round and a-round we go to swing them all a-round.

Round and round we go to swing them all a-round.

go and a-round and a-round and a-round to swing them all a-round we go.

Plink-a plink-a plink-a plink-a plink-a plink-a plink-a plink-a plink-a plink-a plink-a plink-a

Old grey goose come fly-ing home, come fly-ing home, come fly-ing home,

Plunk plunk plunk plunk plunk plunk plunk plunk plunk plunk plunk plunk

**TENOR BASS CHORUS**

# Christmas Comin'

For TB or TTB a cappella

West Indian Carol

Arranged by
EMILY CROCKER

Tenor I
(Opt.)

Tenor II

Bass

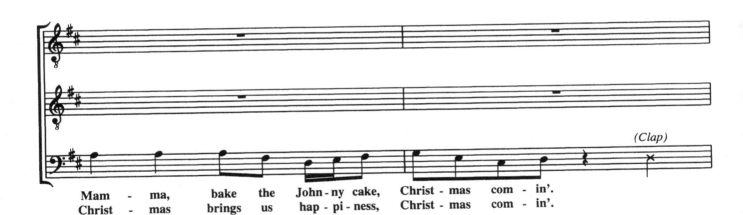

Mam - ma, bake the John-ny cake, Christ - mas com - in'.
Christ - mas brings us hap - pi - ness, Christ - mas com - in'.

Mam - ma, bake the John-ny cake, Christ - mas com - in'.
Christ - mas brings us hap - pi - ness, Christ - mas com - in'.

Mam - ma, bake the John-ny cake, Christ - mas com - in'.
Christ - mas brings us hap - pi - ness, Christ - mas com - in'.

Mam - ma, bake the John-ny cake, Christ - mas com - in'.
Christ - mas brings us hap - pi - ness, Christ - mas com - in'.

Mam - ma, bake the John - ny cake, Christ - mas com - in'.
Christ - mas brings us hap - pi - ness, Christ - mas com - in'.

Mam - ma, bake the John - ny cake, Christ - mas com - in'.
Christ - mas brings us hap - pi - ness, Christ - mas com - in'.

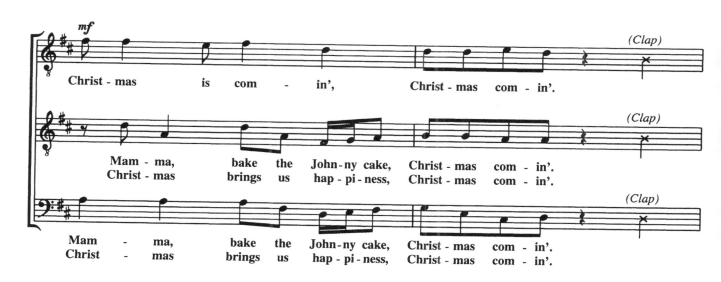

Christ - mas is com - in', Christ - mas com - in'.

Mam - ma, bake the John - ny cake, Christ - mas com - in'.
Christ - mas brings us hap - pi - ness, Christ - mas com - in'.

Mam - ma, bake the John - ny cake, Christ - mas com - in'.
Christ - mas brings us hap - pi - ness, Christ - mas com - in'.

Christ - mas is com - in', Christ - mas com - in'.

Mam - ma, bake the John - ny cake, Christ - mas com - in'.
Christ - mas brings us hap - pi - ness, Christ - mas com - in'.

Mam - ma, bake the John - ny cake, Christ - mas com - in'.
Christ - mas brings us hap - pi - ness, Christ - mas com - in'.

Christ - mas com - in', *(Clap)* Christ - mas com - in', *(Clap)*

Christ - mas com - in', *(Clap)* Christ - mas com - in', *(Clap)*

Christ - mas com - in', *(Clap)* Christ - mas com - in', *(Clap)*

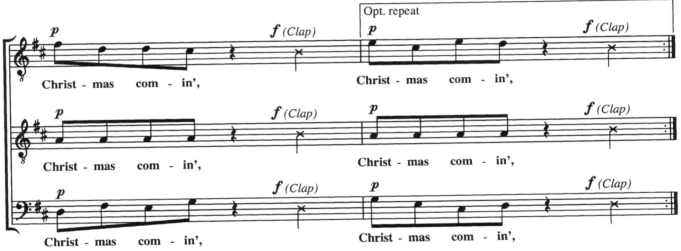

Opt. repeat

Christ - mas com - in', *f (Clap)* Christ - mas com - in', *f (Clap)*

Christ - mas com - in', *f (Clap)* Christ - mas com - in', *f (Clap)*

Christ - mas com - in', *f (Clap)* Christ - mas com - in', *f (Clap)*

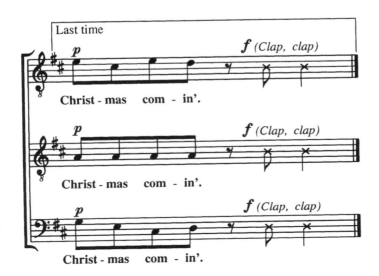

Last time

Christ - mas com - in'. *f (Clap, clap)*

Christ - mas com - in'. *f (Clap, clap)*

Christ - mas com - in'. *f (Clap, clap)*

**MIXED CHORUS**

# Cripple Creek

For SATB and Piano

American Fiddle Tune

Arranged by
EMILY CROCKER

 **POSTURE/BREATH**

1. Stretch your arms overhead, then bend at the waist and stretch toward the floor. Slowly rise up, one vertebra at a time until you are in a standing posture.

2. Rotate your shoulders, first your left, then your right, then both shoulders. Raise your head so that it is in line with the spinal column, and not tilted up or down. Remember to stand in a good singing posture:
   - Stand with feet apart (Is your weight balanced?)
   - Knees unlocked (Can you bend them easily?)
   - Back straight (Are you standing erect comfortably and not stiff?)
   - Head erect (Is your chin level, and not too far up or down?)
   - Rib cage lifted (Is your chest high and able to expand?)
   - Shoulders relaxed (Are they comfortably down, not too far forward or back?)
   - Hands at your side (Are they relaxed and free of tension?)

3. When people are suddenly startled, they usually take a deep natural breath very quickly. Take a "surprised" breath. Notice the action of the *diaphragm*.

4. Imagine that there is an elevator platform at the bottom of your lungs. Drop the platform toward the floor as you inhale. Inhale 4 counts, exhale 4 counts. Repeat with 5, then 6 counts.

### Tone/Registers/Range

Remember the three registers of the voice: *chest*, *middle*, and *head*. Your goal as a singer should be to work to develop a tone quality in which the registers are matched from the bottom of your range to the top. This means that there should not be a dramatic difference between the different registers. In private voice lessons, this is easier to achieve, but conscientious practice in choral rehearsals can produce good results.

**TONE/REGISTERS/RANGE**

⑥

m
oo
ee

Sing on note names or neutral syllables.

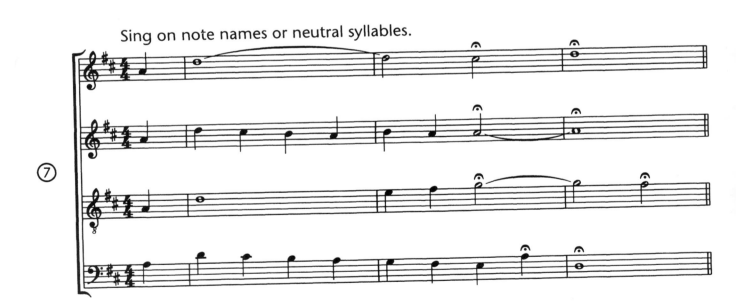

⑦

## KEY OF B♭ MAJOR

The key of B♭ major indicates that the keynote will be B♭. The graphic below shows the B♭ major scale as well as the whole/half step progression that is required for a major scale.

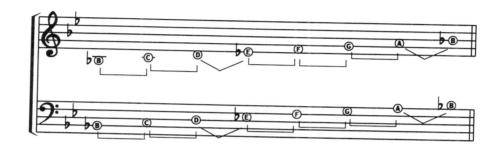

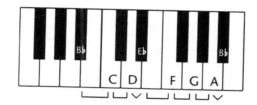

This time, the whole/half step progression requires E♭. If we had written D-E, the interval between these two pitches would have been a whole step rather than the required half step. Thus, the key signature for B♭ major is B♭ and E♭ (in that order).

You'll recall that F major with one flat lies an interval of a fifth *lower* than C major (which has no sharps or flats). B♭ major which has two flats, lies a 5th lower than F major.

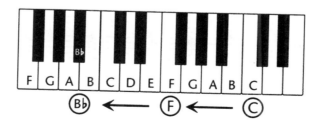

## Check your knowledge!

What is the key signature for B♭ major? For F major? For C major?

B♭ CHORD DRILLS

The Scale

Chord Builders

① I  IV  V  I

②

Chord Drills

③  ④  ⑤

⑥  ⑦

**MELODY DRILLS**

Read each line separately and in any combination.

① (treble clef, 2 flats, 3/4 time — melody)

② (treble clef, 2 flats, 3/4 time — melody)

③ (treble clef, 2 flats, 3/4 time — melody)

④ (treble clef, 2 flats, 3/4 time — melody)

⑤ (treble clef, 2 flats, 3/4 time — melody)

⑥ (bass clef, 2 flats, 3/4 time — melody)

⑦ (bass clef, 2 flats, 3/4 time — melody)

⑧ (bass clef, 2 flats, 3/4 time — melody)

**TREBLE CHORUS**

# Au clair de la lune
## (Clear The Moon)
For SA or SSA a cappella

French Folksong

Arranged by
EMILY CROCKER

**TENOR BASS CHORUS**

# Red River Valley

For TB or TTB a cappella

American Cowboy Song

Arranged by
EMILY CROCKER

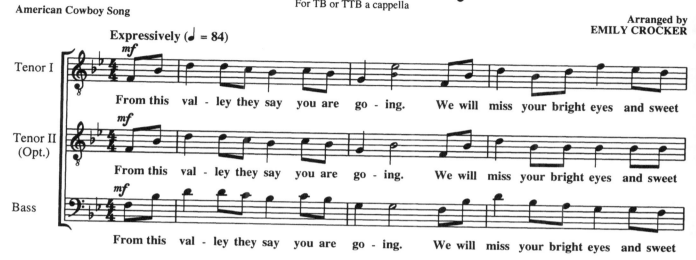

Tenor I

*mf*

From this val - ley they say you are go - ing. We will miss your bright eyes and sweet

Tenor II
(Opt.)

*mf*

From this val - ley they say you are go - ing. We will miss your bright eyes and sweet

Bass

*mf*

From this val - ley they say you are go - ing. We will miss your bright eyes and sweet

smile, for they say you are tak - ing the sun - shine that has

smile, _____ for they say you are tak - ing the sun - shine that has

smile, for they say you are tak - ing the sun - shine that has

*mp*

bright - ened our path for a - while. Come and sit by my side if you

*mp*

bright - ened our path for a - while. Come and sit by my side if you

*mp*

bright - ened our path for a - while. Come and sit by my side if you

**MIXED CHORUS**

# It Was A Lover And His Lass

For SATB a cappella

Text by WILLIAM SHAKESPEARE

Music by JOHN LEAVITT

## POSTURE/BREATH

1. Stretch, then yawn-sigh.

2. As you stand in your best singing posture, concentrate on relaxing and releasing the tension in your body without slumping.
   - Relax your neck and move your head forward and up, so that it is aligned with your spine.
   - Allow your spinal column to lengthen vertically.
   - Balance your weight evenly between your feet, and evenly between the heel and the ball of the feet.
   - Release the tension in your knees.
   - Release the tension in your shoulders.

3. Shape your mouth in an "ah" and inhale while pulling your elbows back. Bring your arms forward as you exhale on a whispered "oo." Repeat several times.

4. Imagine a milkshake as large as the room. "Drink" the air through a large straw.

## Tone/Articulation

**Diphthongs:** (Pronounced DIF-thong)
You are familiar with the five basic vowels for choral singing: ee, eh, ah, oh, oo. As covered in previous chapters, other vowel sounds (ă, ŭ, ĭ, ə and others) are modifications of these basic vowels. A combination of two vowel sounds is called a *diphthong*. Since vowels are the basis of a free and open tone, and a choral sound that is blended and in tune, it is important to learn to sing vowels and diphthongs as an ensemble.

A diphthong consists of two vowel sounds: the *primary* vowel sound and a *secondary* vowel sound. This secondary vowel sound is (usually) at the very end of the diphthong, just before the final consonant or next word or syllable.

For example, the word "I" is really a diphthong using an "ah" and an "ee." The "ee" is a very brief, almost phantom sound at the end of the word.

I = ah_____(ee)

ah

ee

### DIPHTHONGS

Here are some other common diphthongs.  Sing each word on a unison pitch, and concentrate on maintaining the pure, primary vowel sound. Just as you release, place the final secondary vowel sound at the end of the tone.  It should be very understated and unstressed. Can you think of other examples? Can you find examples in the music you are rehearsing?

though = (th)oh_____(oo)

day = (d)eh_____(ee)

joy = (j)aw_____(ee)

Some diphthongs are formed from consonant sounds, and the secondary sound occurs before the primary vowel sound:

you = (ee)oo_____

want = (oo)ah_____(nt)

Practice the following exercises using diphthongs.

⑤

Repeat with:

| I | [ah_____(ee)] |
| why | [(oo)ah_____(ee)] |
| time | [(t)ah_____(eem)] |

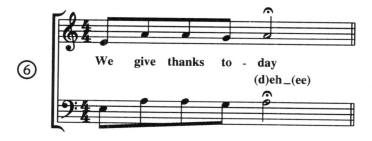

⑥

Repeat with:

Hear us as we pray    [(pr)eh_____(ee)]

Show us now the way    [(oo)eh_____(ee)]

## DIPHTHONG PRACTICE

⑦

Ah, the moon is shin - ing     clear - ly   in  the  night
    [ah(ee)]                                [ah(ee)]

Repeat with:

Yet I stand here
sighing  [(s)ah _____(ing)]
in the pale moonlight
[(l)ah _____(eet)]

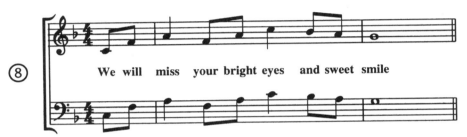

⑧

We  will   miss   your  bright eyes   and sweet smile

bright   [(br)ah _____(eet)]
eyes     [ah _____(eez)]
smile    [(sm)ah _____(eel)]

⑨

Spring  -   time,    ring  -   time
Joy _____     joy _____

time   [(t)ah_____(eem)]
joy    [(j)aw _____(ee)]

⑩

Si - lent,  be  si - lent
Now,  my      la - dy

silent  [(s)ah_____(ee)] - lent
now     [(n)ah _____(oo)]
my      (m)ah _____(ee)]

## NATURAL AND RELATIVE MINOR SCALES

So far the music in this text has been organized around a tonic with a major scale. With the number of keys available, this gives a fair amount of variety. However, composers often write their music on scales with different arrangements of whole/half steps. In addition to the major scale, one of the most common scales is the natural minor scale. Below is listed the *natural minor* scale with the arrangement of whole/half steps.

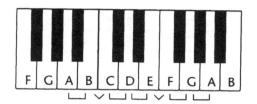

    ⌣ = whole step

    ∨ = half step

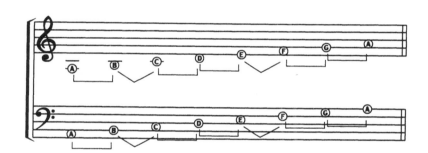

The chief difference between the major and minor scale is the third degree of the scale. In minor, the third degree is a half step lower than the major scale. You will notice this difference in the quality of the sound of the scale. Composers have used minor to suggest a variety of qualities and emotions in music. Minor might be more suggestive of melancholy, sadness, anger, passion, etc.

Listen to your teacher (or another student) play both a major and a minor scale. As a class, make a list of adjectives to describe the two scales. Repeat the exercise with your teacher playing a song in major and one in minor. Describe the emotions you hear and feel in the music.

## NATURAL AND RELATIVE MINOR SCALES

Natural minor scales share the same key signature with a corresponding major scale. These are called relatives. The relative minor is always the sixth degree of the major scale. For example, *C major* has no sharps or flats and *a minor* has no sharps or flats. G major/e minor has one sharp. F major/d minor has one flat.

Here are some major scales with their relative minors. Practice singing each scale:

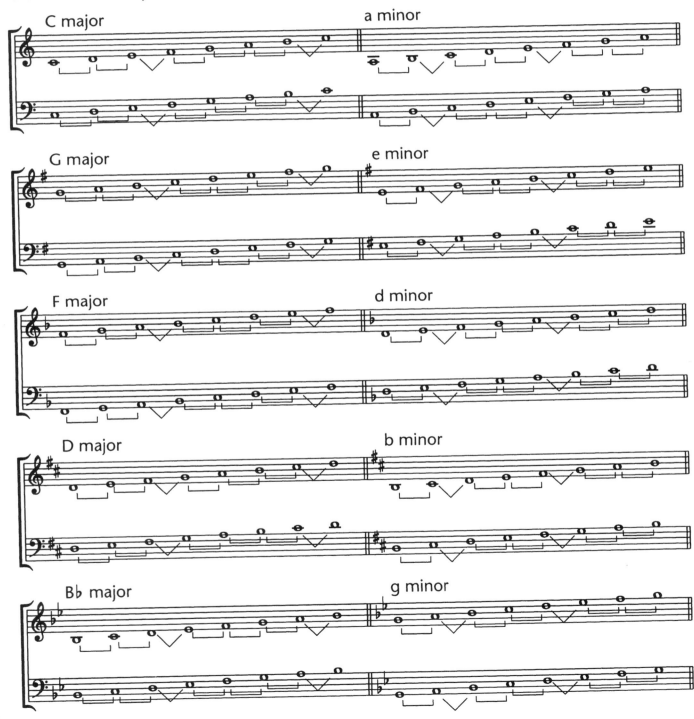

## KEY PRACTICE

When you are preparing to read a new piece of music, how can you determine the key? In addition to looking at the key signature, a good rule of thumb is to look at the beginning and ending notes/chords to find the tonic. Look at the tunes below. Can you decide the key for each example?

## Check your knowledge!

1. What is the arrangement of whole/half steps for a natural minor scale?

2. What is the chief difference between major and minor?

3. What qualities or emotions might be suggested by music in minor?

4. What are relatives? What are the relatives of C, G, F, D major?

5. How can you determine the key for a piece of music?

## NATURAL MINOR

Look at the key signature and determine the key for each exercise before singing.

**TREBLE CHORUS**

# We Give Thanks

For SSA a cappella

Traditional Canon, adapted

Arranged by
EMILY CROCKER

**TENOR BASS CHORUS**

# We Give Thanks

For TTB a cappella

Traditional Canon, adapted

Arranged by
EMILY CROCKER

**MIXED CHORUS**

# Fog

For SATB a cappella

Words by
CARL SANDBURG

Music by
JOHN LEAVITT

si - lent haunch-es ___ and then moves on. Oo ___

si - lent haunch-es ___ and then moves on. Oo ___

Oo ___ and then moves on. Oo ___

Oo ___ and then moves on. Oo ___

*Optional raised third

### POSTURE/BREATH

1. Stretch high overhead. Bend at the waist and gradually stand upright, one vertebra at a time. Nod your head "yes" several times, then "no."

2. Yawn-sigh.

3. Imagine there is a milkshake as large as the room. "Drink" the air through a large straw. Exhale on a yawn-sigh.

4. Sip in air as though you were sipping water. Notice the cool feeling in your throat.

5. Breathe in with your lips in an "oo" shape, then sing the following exercise. Repeat the pattern at different pitch levels, both higher and lower. Open the vowel to an "ah" as you go higher and an "oh" as you go lower.

### Tone/Resonance/Range

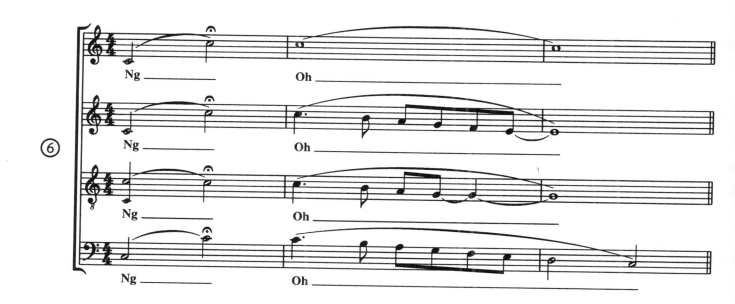

## TONE/ARTICULATION/BLEND

### Articulation

⑦ The good-look-ing cook took a good look. The good-look-ing cook took a good look. The

good-look-ing cook took a good look. The good cook took a look.

### Intonation/Blend (Natural Minor)

Sing the following exercise in unison, then in a round with Voice I holding the last pitch until all voices have reached a unison pitch for tuning. Repeat at different pitch levels.

⑧ meh mah meh    meh mah meh    meh mah meh    meh mah meh

Sing the following melodic exercise in unison and in a canon, with Voice I holding the last pitch until all voices have reached a unison pitch for tuning.

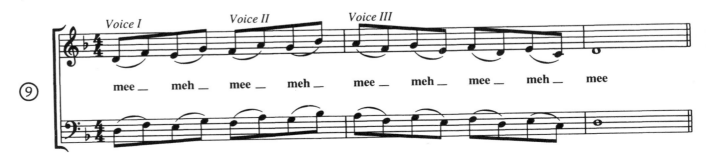

⑨ mee __ meh __ mee __ meh __    mee __ meh __ mee __ meh __ mee

## TIES AND SLURS

You've noticed that occasionally we've used *ties* and *slurs* in music. Ties and slurs appear as curved lines connecting together notes or groups of notes, but they serve very different functions.

A tie connects two notes of the same pitch in order to extend duration. The first note is played or sung and held through the tied second note. See the example below.

A slur is a curved line that connects two or more notes with the purpose to play or sing them smoothly (legato). See the example below.

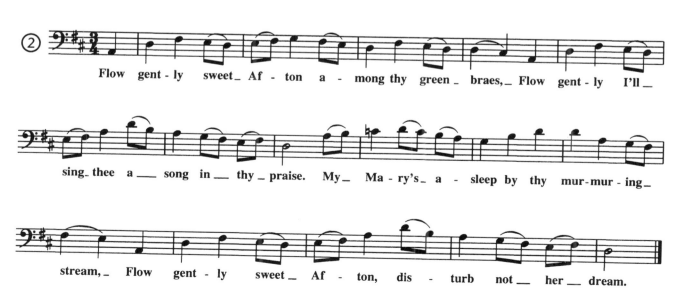

**TIES AND SLURS**

Read each line (clap, tap, or chant).

## Freu dich des Lebens

*2-Part Canon*

Ludwig van Beethoven

Freu dich des Le - bens, freu _____ dich, freu _____
*Joy to your liv - ing, joy _____ to you, _____*

dich des Le - bens, des Le - bens, des Le - bens.
*to your liv - ing, your liv - ing, your liv - ing.*

## DOTTED NOTES AND RHYTHMS

Remember that the duration of a note can be enlarged by adding a dot to the right of the note head. The rule for a dotted note is that the dot receives half the value of the note (or rest).

Sometimes composers prefer to write rhythms that have unequal divisions or subdivisions of the beat. Let's quickly review *beat*, *division*, and *subdivsion* illustrated below.

Dotted rhythms commonly occur as a dotted note followed by a shorter note value as illustrated below.

**Practice** (clap, tap, or chant)

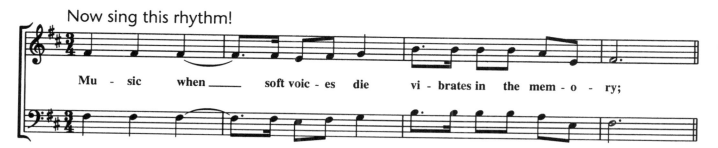

Now sing this rhythm!

Mu - sic when _____ soft voic - es die vi - brates in the mem - o - ry;

## Check your knowledge!

1. What is the difference between a tie and a slur?

2. What is the rule for dotted notes?

3. At which level can dotted notes occur: beat, division, or subdivision? Give examples.

**RHYTHM PRACTICE**

Read each line (clap, tap, or chant).

**SPEECH CHORUS**

# Jeremiah Obadiah

For 2-Part Speech Chorus

Words: Anonymous

Music by
JOHN LEAVITT

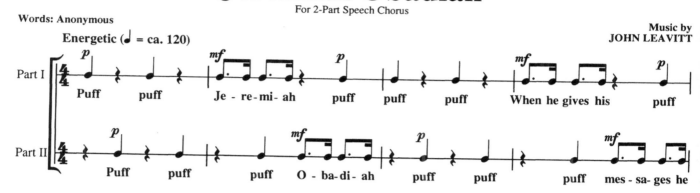

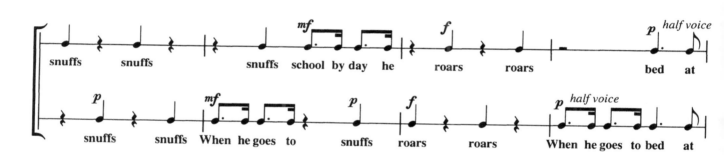

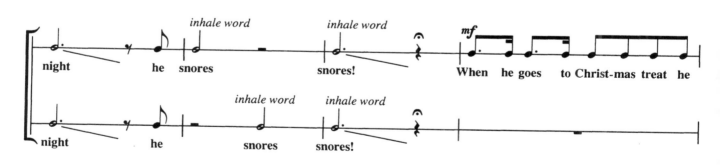

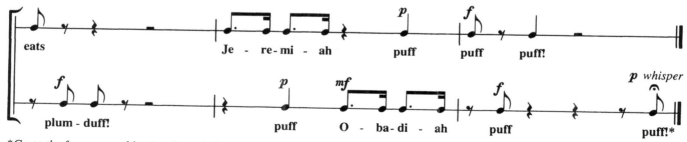

*Go to the f consonant blowing through fermata*

**TREBLE CHORUS**

# Music, When Soft Voices Die

For SA and Piano

Text by
**PERCY BYSSHE SHELLEY (1792-1822)**

Music by
**JOHN LEAVITT**

**TENOR BASS CHORUS**

# Music, When Soft Voices Die
For TB and Piano

Text by
**PERCY BYSSHE SHELLEY (1792-1822)**

Music by
**JOHN LEAVITT**

**MIXED CHORUS**

# O! Mankind
For SATB a cappella

Text: 15th Century Anonymous

Music by
**EMILY CROCKER**

*Opt. raised 3rd

## COMPREHENSIVE REVIEW

1. Describe the steps to a good singing posture.

2. How does good posture affect singing?

3. How does an expanded rib cage affect breathing?

4. List the five basic vowels. Describe the basic formation of each.

5. What is the general rule for producing vowel sounds in addition to the five basic vowels?

6. What is the *neutral* vowel?

7. Why do we need *articulation* in singing? What are the *articulators*?

8. What does *breath support* mean?

9. Describe the movement of the diaphragm, the intercostal muscles, the abdomen, and the lungs during breathing.

10. What is the source of vocal tone? What is it popularly called?

11. How do the vocal folds produce sound?

12. What are the three registers of the singing voice?

13. What is *falsetto*?

14. What is *resonance* in singing?

15. How does the *soft palate* affect resonance?

16. Describe techniques to correct a nasal tone quality.

17. What is a *diphthong*? Describe how to sing a diphthong.

## COMPREHENSIVE REVIEW

### Check your knowledge!

1. What is rhythm?

2. How many half notes equal the same duration as a whole note?

3. How many quarter notes equal the same duration as a half note? As a whole note?

4. How many lines and spaces does a staff have?

5. Give both names for the clefs we've learned and describe them.

6. Name the pitch which may be written on its own little line in either clef.

7. When treble clef notes are written in the bass clef or bass clef notes are written in treble clef, they use additional little lines as in #6. What are these lines called?

8. What are the vertical lines that divide a staff into smaller sections?

9. Name the smaller divided sections of a staff.

10. How can you tell the end of a section or piece of music?

11. Describe *meter*.

12. What is the name for the numbers that identify the meter?

13. Describe the following meters: $\frac{4}{4}$, $\frac{3}{4}$, $\frac{2}{4}$

14. What is another name for musical notes?

15. Define *scale*. What is the Italian word for *scale* and its definition?

16. Describe *key*. Describe *keynote*.

17. What is the difference between a *whole step* and a *half step*?

18. What is a *major scale*?

19. What is the order of whole/half steps in a major scale?

20. What is a slur?

21. Where does the word *pianoforte* come from and what does it mean?

### COMPREHENSIVE REVIEW

22. Describe *f*  *p*  *mf*  *mp*. What are these signs called?

23. What is an octave?

24. Define *soprano, alto, tenor, bass*.

25. What is an *interval*? What is the difference between *melodic* and *harmonic* intervals?

26. What is a chord?

27. How many tones are needed to form a chord?

28. What is the difference between a *chord* and a *triad*?

29. What is another name for *keynote*?

30. On which tone of the major scale is a *tonic chord* built?

31. Describe the key signature for C, G, and F major.

32. How many beat(s) does an eighth note receive in a meter of $\frac{4}{4}$ ?

33. What number of eighth notes equals the duration of a quarter note? A half note? A whole note?

34. What is a *downbeat*?

35. What beats are stressed in $\frac{4}{4}$ meter? In $\frac{3}{4}$ meter? In $\frac{2}{4}$ meter?

36. What is the dotted note rule?

37. How many beats does a half note receive in $\frac{4}{4}$ meter? A dotted half note?

38. On what degree of the major scale is the *dominant* chord built? The *subdominant* chord?

39. Give a description of the relationship between *tonic* and *dominant* chords.

40. Describe the key signature for D and B♭ major.

41. How many sixteenth notes equal an eighth note? A quarter note? A half note? A whole note?

42. In $\frac{2}{4}$ meter, which note represents the beat? The division? The subdivision?

43. What is the arrangement of whole/half steps for *natural minor*?

44. What are the *relative* minors for C, G, D, F, and B♭ major?

45. What qualities or emotions might be suggested by music in a minor key? In a major key?

**TREBLE CHORUS**

# Come Follow

For SSA a cappella

Traditional English

Arranged by
EMILY CROCKER

**TENOR BASS CHORUS**

# The Old Brass Wagon
For TTB a cappella

American Dance Song

Arranged by
EMILY CROCKER

**MIXED CHORUS**

# Sing a Song of Sixpence

For SATB and Piano

Traditional Words and Melody

Arranged by
JOHN LEAVITT

210

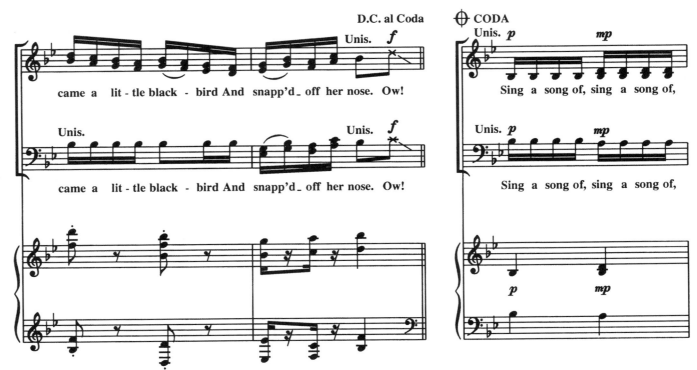

 **SOLFEGE**

(Movable "do")
"Do" changes as the key changes.

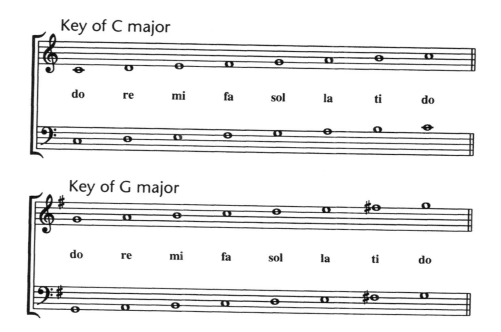

Movable "do" — Accidentals (in all keys)

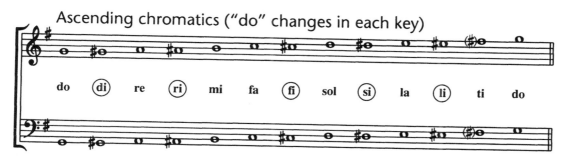

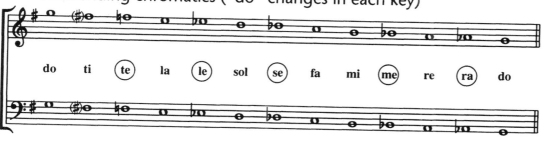

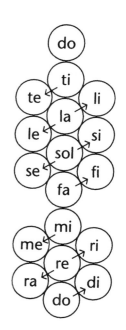

## SOLFEGE

(Fixed "do")
"Do" is C and the pitch syllables remain fixed no matter what the key.

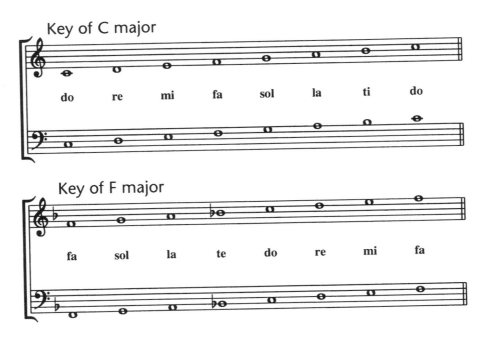

Fixed "do"
Accidentals are fixed as follows:

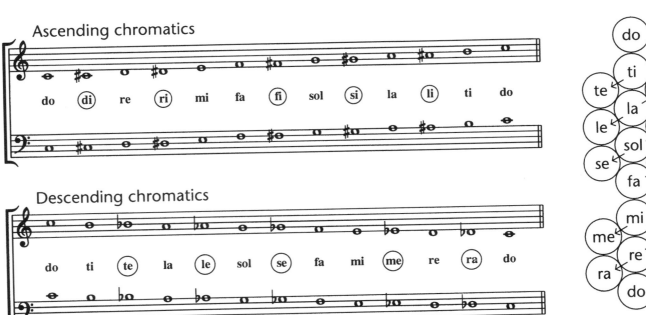

 **NUMBERS**

Numbers (pitch)
Like movable "do," the "1" changes with each key.

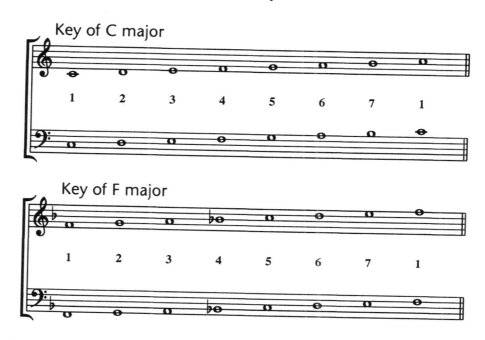

Accidentals can be performed either by singing the number but raising or lowering the pitch by a half step, or by singing the word "sharp" or "flat" before the number as a grace note.

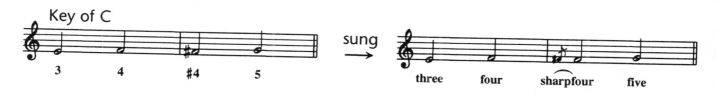

## COUNTING SYSTEMS - SIMPLE METER

There are several systems in use which are quite effective. Here are three:

|  Kodály | Traditional | Eastman |
| --- | --- | --- |
| (Beat) 4/4 ♩ ♩ ♩ ♩ <br> ta  ta  ta  ta | 4/4 ♩ ♩ ♩ ♩ <br> 1  2  3  4 | 4/4 ♩ ♩ ♩ ♩ <br> 1  2  3  4 |
| (Beat) 4/4 ♩ ____ ♩ ____ <br> ta _____ ta _____ | 4/4 <br> 1 _____ 3 _____ | 4/4 <br> 1 _____ 3 _____ |
| (Beat) 4/4 o <br> ta _____ | 4/4 o <br> 1 _____ | 4/4 o <br> 1 _____ |
| (Beat) 4/4 <br> ti ti ti ti ti ti ti ti | 4/4 <br> 1 & 2 & 3 & 4 & | 4/4 <br> 1 te 2 te 3 te 4 te |
| (Beat) 4/4 <br> ti ri ti ri ti ri ti ri ti ri ti ri ti ri ti ri | 4/4 <br> 1 e & a 2 e & a 3 e & a 4 e & a | 4/4 <br> 1 ta te ta 2 ta te ta 3 ta te ta 4 ta te ta |
| (Beat) 4/4 <br> ti ti ri ti ti ri ti ti ri ti ti ri | 4/4 <br> 1 & a 2 & a 3 & a 4 & a | 4/4 <br> 1 te ta 2 te ta 3 te ta 4 te ta |

## COUNTING SYSTEMS

| Kodály | Traditional | Eastman |
|---|---|---|
| ti ri ti  ti ri ti  ti ri ti  ti ri ti | 1 e &  2 e &  3 e &  4 e & | 1 ta te  2 ta te  3 ta te  4 ta te |
| ta _____ ta | 1 _____ 4 | 1 _____ 4 |
| ta  i  ti  ta  i  ti | 1 _____ &  3 _____ & | 1 _____ te  3 _____ te |
| tim ri tim  ri tim  ri tim  ri | 1  a 2  a 3  a 4  a | 1  ta 2  ta 3  ta 4  ta |
| tir im  tir im  tir im  tir im | 1 e  2 e  3 e  4 e | 1 ta  2 ta  3 ta  4 ta |
| ta  ta  ta  ta ___ ta ___ | 1  2  3  4 ___ 3 | 1  2  3  4 ___ 3 ___ |
| ta  ta _____ ta | 1  2 _____ 4 | 1  2 _____ 4 |
| syn - co - pa syn - co - pa (or ti  ta  ti) | 1  & ___ & 3  & ___ & | 1  te ___ te 3  te ___ te |
| tir im  ri tir im  ri tir im  ri tir im  ri | 1 e  a 2 e  a 3 e  a 4 e  a | 1 ta  ta 2 ta  ta 3 ta  ta 4 ta  ta |

## OTHER SIMPLE METERS

Adapt the information from the charts on pages 216-217 to apply to music in other simple meters.

**Simple Meters:** Simple meters are based upon the note which receives the beat, i.e. $\frac{4}{4}$ meter is based upon the quarter note receiving the beat.

2 = 2 beats per measure ( ♪ ♪ )
8 = The eighth note ( ♪ ) receives the beat

3 = 3 beats per measure ( ♪ ♪ ♪ )
8 = The eighth note ( ♪ ) receives the beat

4 = 4 beats per measure ( ♪ ♪ ♪ ♪ )
8 = The eighth note ( ♪ ) receives the beat

2 = 2 beats per measure ( ♩ ♩ )
2 = The half note ( ♩ ) receives the beat   (Note: sometimes written as ¢ "cut time")

3 = 3 beats per measure ( ♩ ♩ ♩ )
2 = The half note ( ♩ ) receives the beat

4 = 4 beats per measure ( ♩ ♩ ♩ ♩ )
2 = The half note ( ♩ ) receives the beat.

## E COMPOUND METER

Kodály | Traditional | Eastman

(Beat)
ti ti ti ti ti ti
(or tri - ple - ti tri - ple - ti)
1 2 3 4 5 6
1 la li 2 la li
(Beat)
ta ti ta ti
1 3 4 6
1 li 2 li
(Beat)
ta i ta i
1 4
1 2
(Beat)
ta
1
1

## OTHER COMPOUND METERS

Adapt the information from the above charts to apply to music in other compound meters.

Compound Meters: Compound meters are meters which have a multiple of 3, such as 6 or 9 (but not 3 itself). Unlike simple meter which reflects the note that receives the beat, compound meter reflects the note that receives the division.

To determine the note that receives the beat, add three divisions together. For example:

6 = 6 divisions to the measure (2 groups of 3)
8 = The eighth note receives the division
(the dotted quarter receives the beat)

9 = 9 divisions to the measure (3 groups of 3)
8 = The eighth note receives the division
(the dotted quarter receives the beat)

12 = 12 divisions to the measure (4 groups of 3)
4 = The quarter note receives the division
(the dotted half note receives the beat)

An exception to this compound meter rule is when the music occurs at a slow tempo, then the music is felt in beats, rather than divisions.

## RHYTHM DRILLS

### Simple Meter

The rhythmic, melodic, and harmonic exercises on the following pages are included for reference or drill as needed.

### Beat, Division, and Subdivision

Clap, tap, or chant each line

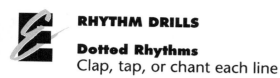

**RHYTHM DRILLS**

**Dotted Rhythms**

Clap, tap, or chant each line

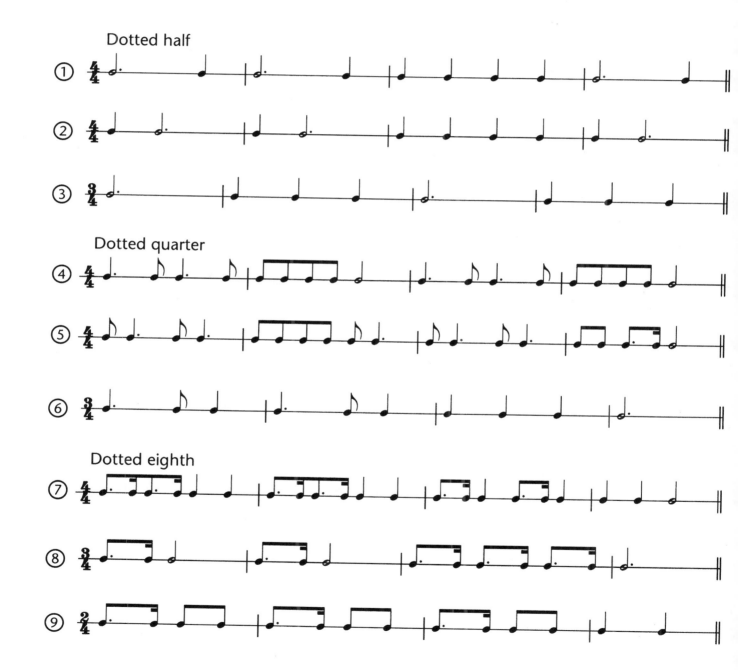

## RHYTHM DRILLS

### Compound Meter

Clap, tap, or chant each line.
What note gets the beat? The division?

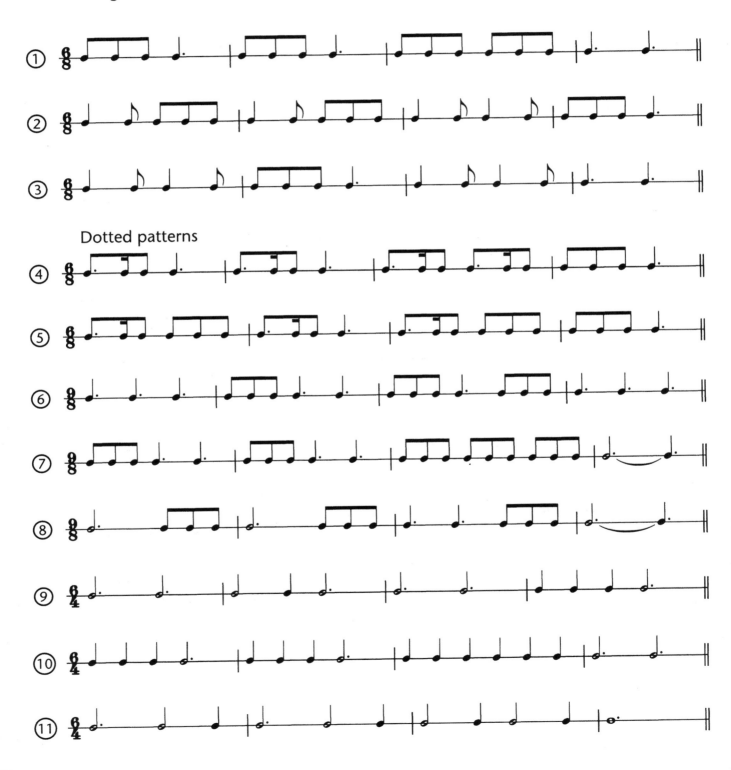

Dotted patterns

**PITCH DRILLS**

**Key of A Major**

The Scale

Interval Drills

Chord Drills

Melodic Drill

**PITCH DRILLS**

**Key of E Flat Major**

The Scale

Interval Drills

Chord Drills

Melodic Drill

# APPENDIX

## THE CIRCLE OF FIFTHS

There is a pattern in the relationships of sharp and flat keys. The relationship is based upon the interval of a fifth separating adjacent keys. See the keyboard graphic below:

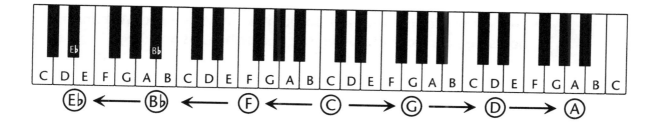

Sometimes a memory aid is used to recall these relationships. It is called the *Circle of Fifths*. Notice the sharps and flats as well as the keys are separated by the distance of a fifth. (Sharps are added by going up a fifth, flats are added by going down a fifth.)

Sharp order: F#, C#, G#, D#, A#, E#, B#

Flat order: B♭, E♭, A♭, D♭, G♭, C♭, F♭

(You'll also notice the order of sharps and flats are exact mirrors of each other.)

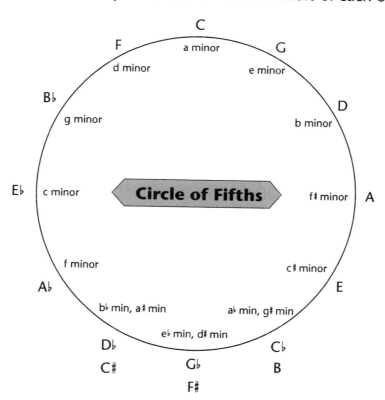

## ABOUT THE AUTHORS

**EMILY HOLT CROCKER** is a native Texan and was a professional educator for 15 years. She taught all levels of choral music, specializing in middle school/junior high, where her choirs received numerous superior ratings in concert and sight-reading competitions. In 1989, she joined the music publishing industry and in 1992 was named Director of Choral Publications for Hal Leonard Corporation in Milwaukee, Wisconsin. She holds degrees from the University of North Texas and Texas Woman's University and has done additional post-graduate work at the University of North Texas, where she was assistant conductor of the A Cappella Choir and taught music education.

She is the founder and director of the Milwaukee Children's Choir, a group that was organized in 1994 and is sponsored by the Milwaukee Chamber Orchestra.

Ms. Crocker is known nationally as one of the premier choral writers specializing in music for young choirs. She has over one hundred works currently in print and since 1986 has been awarded ASCAP special awards for Educational and Concert music. In addition to her responsibilities at Hal Leonard, she maintains a busy guest conducting, workshop, and writing schedule each year.

**JOHN LEAVITT** is a Kansas native, born and raised in Leavenworth, Kansas. He completed doctoral work in Choral Conducting at the University of Missouri-Kansas City Conservatory of Music.

His undergraduate work is in music education from Emporia State University. After graduation, Dr. Leavitt moved to Wichita, Kansas where he worked in television for five years. At Wichita State University, he pursued a Master of Music degree in piano performance with significant study in composition.

While in Wichita, he directed the parish music program at Immanuel Lutheran Church and served on the faculty at Friends University where he won the faculty award for teaching excellence in 1989. In the fall of 1992, Dr. Leavitt accepted a one year teaching appointment with Concordia College in Edmonton, Alberta, Canada, where he was director of choral activities and assistant professor of music.

Returning in 1993 to Wichita, he now devotes himself to full-time composing and conducting. He is the artistic director and conductor of a professionally trained vocal ensemble known as The Master Arts Chorale and an associated Children's Choir, The Master Arts Youth Chorale.

Dr. Leavitt's works receive wide acclaim and he has received ASCAP awards since 1991. In addition to his busy guest conducting and workshop schedule, he writes many commissioned works each year.